Residential Renewal in the Urban Core

An analysis of the demand for housing
in Center City Philadelphia, 1957 to 1970,
with reference to the
Washington Square East Redevelopment Area

by
Chester Rapkin
and
William G. Grigsby

Philadelphia · University of Pennsylvania Press

Throughout the United States, a massive program of city rebuilding is in progress. Although the effort is still in its early stages, both locally and nationally, the breadth of its scope is unmistakable. Even now, several hundred cities throughout the land display new homes, new public and private nonresidential buildings, restored historical monuments, and graceful open spaces, on sites that short years ago produced little but dismay. The work in process will enlarge these achievements many times over, and the plans for even the foreseeable future will materially improve the entire urban environment.

The city of Philadelphia, an unquestioned leader in the field of city rebuilding, is the subject of the present volume. Specifically, this study is devoted to a demonstration of the means whereby economic, sociological, and market analysis can be employed as a material aid in planning for urban renewal. The authors have addressed themselves to the problem of estimating the demand for housing accommodations of the type that will be found in most renewal projects in central cities throughout the country. In downtown Philadelphia they have studied the kinds of people who reside in higher priced housing accommodations and the changing preference of these households, within the larger structure of housing demand for the entire metropolitan region. In the process they have uncovered many facts that have significant planning implications that go beyond the immediate purposes of the study. The basic estimates reported here have provided guides to public officials concerned with formulating planning goals and objectives for the rebuilding of the city.

Although this study deals with but a single city, the cross currents that it investigates are characteristic of the larger American metropolis, and the methods that are employed are applicable to other similar areas. It is hoped, therefore, that this work will contribute to the efforts to enhance the vitality of the central sections of American urban centers.

Residential Renewal in the Urban Core

Institute for Urban Studies
University of Pennsylvania

William L. C. Wheaton
Director

This study was prepared under contract with
THE REDEVELOPMENT AUTHORITY
OF THE CITY OF PHILADELPHIA

FOREWORD

Without question the city of Philadelphia has assumed a position of leadership in the massive program of city rebuilding that is now in progress throughout the United States. Although the program is still in its early stages, both locally and nationally, the breadth of its scope is unmistakable. Even at this point several hundred cities in all corners of the land can display new homes, new public and private nonresidential buildings, restored historical monuments, and graceful open spaces, on sites that short years ago produced little but dismay. The work in process will enlarge these achievements many times over, and the plans for even the foreseeable future will materially improve the entire urban environment.

We can now look forward to an acceleration in the pace of accomplishment. Much of the initial stage of the rebuilding process was devoted to devising, testing, and developing the necessary legal, governmental, and business tools, and these instruments have now reached a workable stage. Moreover, the scope of the process has been enlarged to include the conservation and rehabilitation of existing structures, as well as clearance and reconstruction. Of greater importance, perhaps, is the fact that the possibilities inherent in our cities have captured

7

the imagination of the people and have given them a vision that goes beyond the physical structures themselves.

In Philadelphia the renewal program at present includes seventeen projects varying widely in character and in scope. Some of the projects have been completed; others are under construction or in the planning stages. The Washington Square East Redevelopment Project, with which this study is concerned, is being undertaken by the Philadelphia Redevelopment Authority in conformity with plans of the City Planning Commission. It is one of several projects in downtown Philadelphia that together comprise a vast program encompassing the entire central area from Lombard to Spring Garden Street and from the Delaware to the Schuylkill River. It is estimated that public and private investments of approximately one billion dollars will be required to implement the twenty to twenty-five year plan for center city. Upon its successful completion, Philadelphia will possess a central core that is truly articulated with the economic and social functions of a modern metropolis.

The Washington Square East Redevelopment Area (better known as Society Hill) is a section of old Philadelphia that is rich in the symbols of American tradition. One of its boundaries is Independence Square, and in the surrounding area lived many of the men and women who helped form the republic. Thus, the revivification of this area is bound to have meaning and influence far beyond its immediate scope.

The body of this report is devoted to an analysis of the demand for housing in the redevelopment area after reconstruction. Its purpose is to provide the officials of government concerned with the rebuilding of the city with data on the current state of the market and its long-term potentialities. The study itself was commissioned by the Philadelphia Redevelopment Authority and conducted by the Institute for Urban Studies, University of Pennsylvania. Because of the unusual type of market and the strategic importance of the area in the rejuvenation of center city, the Authority felt a

CITY OF PHILADELPHIA
AND ITS CENTRAL DISTRICT.

REDEVELOPMENT AREAS

SOCIETY HILL REDEVELOPMENT AREA

------ BOUNDARY - CENTRAL DISTRICT

MILES

particular need for such an analysis. Even though formal housing market studies have been conducted throughout the country for well over two decades, most of the work has been on a city or metropolitan area basis and very little on the more difficult problem of analysing the market in smaller areas.

The conduct of this study has been greatly facilitated and expedited by the fact that the Institute had undertaken a study of potential housing demand in the Eastwick Redevelopment Area. The Eastwick study included a sample survey of Philadelphia population and households and numerous estimates and projections which also served as a basis for many of the Society Hill calculations. The accumulated body of data and experience made possible economies of time and cost to the Authority.

In undertaking our work we have been repeatedly heartened and gratified by the generous and friendly fashion in which busy people have given us their time, shared their experiences, and made available their statistical records. We, therefore, welcome this traditional opportunity to thank the following people for their invaluable aid:

To: Martin Meyerson, Williams Professor of City Planning, Harvard University, and Vice-President of American Council to Improve Our Neighborhoods (ACTION), and to *Fortune* magazine for permission to utilize the results of their field survey of the residents of downtown Philadelphia.

To: Robert Adelsker, Jerome Blum, John L. Graham, Jr., Harry K. Madway, C. E. Moynihan, Dr. Joseph J. Noonan, Clifford Pascoe, and T. E. Whitehead for sharing their experiences with us in the rental and management of downtown apartments and for facilitating interviews with apartment residents.

To: John J. Herd, Milton Hollander, Earl James, and Charles P. LaGrossa for providing us with a better understanding of the forces at work in the rejuvenation of downtown Philadelphia and for giving us valuable insights into the market for single family homes and the problems of rehabilitation.

To: Morton Baratz, Robert O. Crockett, Mason C. Doan, Herbert Gans, Frank S. Kristof, Louis Loewenstein, William H. Ludlow, Sherman J. Maisel, William W. Nash, Una K. Oberman, Kirk R. Petshek, Arthur T. Row, John E. Teller, David A. Wallace, Robert C. Weaver, and Louis Winnick for helpful comment and constructive criticism of early drafts of this study.

To: Lillian W. Israel for an outstanding job of interviewing and Grace Milgram for material aid in preparing the final manuscript for publication.

To: Webb & Knapp Inc. for permission to use an artist's rendering of redeveloped Society Hill, and Attilio Bergamasco for preparing the necessary maps.

To: Gwendolyn Blanks, Promila Coelho, Herbert Kay, Richard Loewald, Barbara Siegle, and Thomas Taylor for research and secretarial assistance, and good humor and diligent effort throughout the project.

To: More than 500 Philadelphia families who gave up a portion of their leisure time to be interviewed.

And To: Professor William L. C. Wheaton, Director of the Institute for Urban Studies, for assisting us in the original conception of this study and for his unfailing encouragement and incisive comments.

C. R.

W. G. G.

CONTENTS

13

135275

TABLES

17

APPENDIX TABLES

Residential Renewal in the Urban Core

I

Introduction: The Area, the Plan, and the Method of Analysis

It is almost self-evident that the likelihood of success of any planning endeavor is enhanced by the extent to which it conforms with and utilizes existing economic currents. Perhaps economic considerations are nowhere more strategic than in the renewal and redevelopment undertakings that now loom so large and dramatically in the planning programs of urban areas. Renewal or redevelopment by its very nature, in part, runs counter to trend, and it is therefore essential to determine whether the specific objectives that cannot or will not materialize in the normal course of market development have the economic potentiality necessary for realization.

Economic feasibility depends largely upon the market potential for the facilities to be provided in the renewal area. The magnitude of demand will determine the rate at which the new improvements will be absorbed. Were it possible to wait long enough, given any positive level of demand, the entire supply would ultimately be rented or sold. But unoccupied space is not costless—either in an economic or social sense. Operating expense and debt service continue after reconstruction; and families and business firms are forced to move prior to renewal. Thus the essential significance of a demand estimate lies in the aid that it provides in formulating a sound renewal plan and in specifying a construction schedule for the various types of facilities contemplated.

This study is concerned with estimating the future demand for housing in the central core of Philadelphia, in order to adjudge the dimension of the market for dwelling units to be constructed in the Society Hill Renewal Area. Although it deals with but a single city, the cross currents that it investigates are characteristic of the larger American metropolis, and the methods that are employed may be applicable to other similar areas. It is hoped, therefore, that this work will contribute to the widespread efforts to restore vitality to the declining central sections of our urban centers.

To put the analysis in perspective, this chapter is devoted to a brief history and description of the area and to the plan for the future. These expository materials are then followed by a general statement of the methods pursued in the study and to a preview of the contents of the remainder of the report.

THE AREA

Society Hill is a section of the Old City. These two sobriquets indicate the fact that the redevelopment area is one of the earliest places of settlement in Philadelphia and notes its association with the early Society of Free Traders. Scattered throughout the district are many buildings of historical significance, some of which are symbols of the republic. There yet remains a sprinkling of fine homes of Philadelphia's first families, and several are still occupied by their descendants. For a period this section was among the most fashionable in the city, but throughout this interval it has also been an area of contrasts. In the narrow back alleys behind the handsome structures were huddled smaller buildings housing servants and laborers. As early as the colonial era and in the first days of the nation, the streets to the south of the Old City were lined with the homes of a growing number of freedmen who formed the first center of Negro population in Philadelphia.

Approximately a century ago, the elite began to drift westward as the city expanded. For a time they moved north as well, settling temporarily in the vicinity of Logan Circle, but by the late nineteenth century they had definitely established themselves in the Rittenhouse Square area. Society Hill, in the meantime, passed to families lower on the income and social scale, many of whom were immigrants from central and south Europe.

At the same time the area began to suffer from the scattered growth of nonresidential uses. To the east, docks and warehouses expanded and the wholesale food distribution center assumed regional proportions. Office buildings of the old financial and insurance district grew up on the streets adjoining State House Row. Farther to the north, Market Street continued to develop as the center of retail trade for the city while South Street, some half-mile removed, formed the axis of what at one time was the largest Jewish shopping center in Philadelphia. Today, it is largely isolated from the Jewish residents who have moved to scattered areas throughout the region.

From 1920 to 1940, both Society Hill and Rittenhouse Square experienced further change as middle and upper income families moved to outlying locations. Vacated single family structures were placed in other types of residential, and in nonresidential, use. In the Rittenhouse Square area conversions were primarily to professional offices and to a limited number of small apartments. In Society Hill, the conversions tended to be to commercial and industrial use, and also to rooming houses.

As early as the 1920's, efforts were made to rehabilitate sections of the center city in such places as Elfreth's Alley and Camac Street. It was not until the 1940's, however, that rehabilitation exceeded token levels. Largely limited to the swath between Walnut and Pine, it has occurred principally in blocks west of Ninth Street which have now regained a considerable measure of their former charm.

Residential renewal has been accompanied by changes in other land uses as well. The closing of the Camden Ferry in 1952 hastened the general westward movement of retail trade. The demolition of the Chinese Wall removed a blight and a barrier, and made possible the release of a major new development that stimulated the area in other ways: employees in the new office buildings increased housing demand; the construction itself reconfirmed the westward movement of the city's core; and the quality and appearance of the new structures improved the status of the area.

East of Ninth Street to the Delaware River, relatively few units have been rehabilitated or restored, but the number has been severely limited by the blighted environment, particularly the old Dock Street market. Interest in the area has been revived, however, by the restoration of Independence Hall, the construction of the Mall, and by the activities of civic groups. The introduction of private rehabilitation indicates the basic strength of the area, but without public redevelopment there is little likelihood that its full potentialities can be realized.

In a sense Society Hill is a classic renewal area. Despite its excellent location, the value of the land is depressed by the heavy hand of blight. Five out of six residential structures are substandard. Land coverage is excessive, ranging from 60 to 100 per cent. Many commercial and industrial structures occupy the entire lot from street to street, and most residential buildings are singularly devoid of usable open space. Land uses are unrelated and incompatible. Retail trade is too diffuse and the scattered shops make no provision for off-street parking or loading. Many factory buildings are obsolete. The street system, the schools, the recreational facilities, and other community services all are sadly deficient; and as one would expect from this array of defects, sections of the area are abysmally ugly.

What makes this area propitious for renewal are not its liabilities, but its assets, many of which have already been enumerated. Located in the heart of the city, it is directly accessible to all of the employment, educational, and recreational opportunities, as well as to the variety of goods and services that the central district of a metropolis can offer. It borders on the

Delaware River, an advantage that has been pre-empted by industry for too long a time. In addition to this inventory of physical assets, the area has unequalled values and associations by virtue of its role in American history.

THE RENEWAL PLAN

The Washington Square East Redevelopment Area contains 127 acres. It is bounded by Walnut Street on the north, Delaware Avenue on the east, Lombard Street on the south, and Seventh Street, South Washington Square, and Sixth Street on the west. The plan for the area has several objectives which include the clearance of the old produce market, the preservation of the historical and architectural significance of the area, and the development of a residential neighborhood. About one-half of the area will be acquired for clearance and substantial reconstruction. A major portion of the clearance area will be devoted to high rise apartments and new and rehabilitated structures. Buildings of historic significance will, of course, be preserved as will most of the commercial structures along Walnut Street. A large share of the buildings, most of which are located south of Spruce Street, will remain in the hands of private owners who will be encouraged to carry out voluntary rehabilitation in harmony with the plan for the whole area.

The residential section of the renewal plan provides for approximately 2,000 new apartment units mostly in multi-story buildings, the bulk of which will be concentrated in the Dock Street area and the remainder distributed among other locations. In addition, approximately 130 new single family units will be erected and about 300 existing homes reconstructed as private residences. Another 100 structures will be converted into 450 to 500 apartment units. Greenways and institutional, community, and commercial facilities will complete the development.

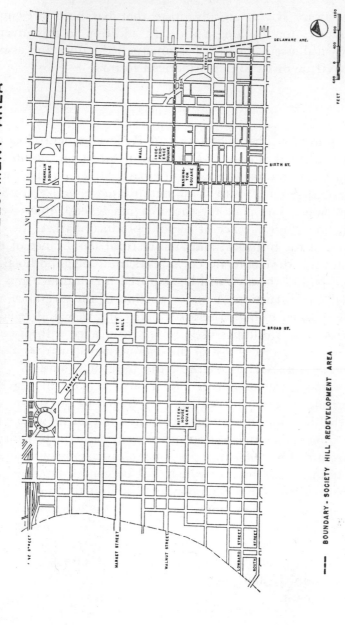

CENTRAL DISTRICT
AND THE SOCIETY HILL REDEVELOPMENT AREA

--- BOUNDARY - SOCIETY HILL REDEVELOPMENT AREA

THE METHOD OF ANALYSIS

To be useful, the schedule of potential demand must, of course, be expressed in terms that approximate as closely as possible the quality and price of the new units. Within the limits of acceptable quality standards, minimum price or rent levels are set by building costs, financial terms, and operating expenses. The extent to which price or rent levels can be reduced by lowering the resale value of the land is limited because official policy requires that the land be sold to the redeveloper at a price economically consistent with the new use, an amount that falls within a very narrow range of estimate.

The final estimates presented in this study are the culmination of a process of reduction in which total housing demand is successively subdivided to focus on those households, which by virtue of their family type, age of household head, income, place of employment of the principal wage earner, or personal preferences, fall within the group from which the occupants of the new units will be drawn. A second stage of the process, fraught with more uncertainties than the first, consists of a series of adjustments that take into account such matters as projected changes in income and in the distribution of employment as between the core of the city and remaining sections of the metropolitan area. The basic data for these phases of the work were drawn from field surveys, one which sampled households in the entire Philadelphia Standard Metropolitan Area and two others that concentrated on the residents of the more distinguished modern apartment houses, particularly those located in the downtown area, as well as the occupants of rehabilitated single family units. An account of these surveys is given elsewhere in this report.

Because of the significance attached to the success of the project in its initial stages, attention was also devoted to appraising the current status of the market for the type of units proposed for Society Hill. Owners, managers, realtors, and builders were interviewed and their experiences collected and collated. A vacancy survey was conducted early in 1958 and conveyance, construction, and assessment records were examined for recent trends.

CONTENTS OF THE REPORT

The following chapter of this report provides a general setting for the local analysis by recounting some of the salient housing market developments in the metropolitan area during the past decade. The ensuing three chapters contain the heart of the matter. They consist of a full presentation of the data, the methods and techniques of analysis, and the pertinent estimates of long-term demand for high and moderate priced apartments and for single family owner occupied units, be they rehabilitated or newly constructed units. For those who are impatient with details, a final chapter has been prepared which summarizes the major findings of the study, stripped of the qualifications which surround them earlier in the volume.

II

Recent Developments in the Housing Market[1]

At the end of 1957 Philadelphia could look back on a decade of accomplishment in the field of housing. The stock in both the city and suburbs had shown substantial growth. The incidence of home ownership had increased dramatically to include over 60 per cent of all households. There was a discernible shift in the preference of Philadelphians in the direction of better living accommodations and a general rise in the quality of all units in the housing supply. It is now evident, however, that the volume of output and sales reached a peak in 1955. Although some of the decline observed since that time has undoubtedly been due to stringency in the home mortgage market, a condition that has pervaded residential financing in all sections of the country, there are indications of a contraction in the underlying factors that generate housing demand. The pace of immigration and of new household formation has slackened, and the mass home purchases of recent years have reduced much of the urgent need for shelter.

The following pages are devoted to a presentation of some of the highlights of the market developments of the past decade. In a sense these conditions constituted the economic setting at the time that the Washington Square East redevelopment proposal was put on the drawing boards.

NEW CONSTRUCTION

Between 1950 and the end of 1956 new construction added approximately 235,000 dwelling units to the stock of housing in

[1] Except where otherwise noted, the information presented in this chapter is from unpublished special tabulations of the *1956 National Housing Inventory*, U.S. Bureau of the Census.

the Philadelphia Standard Metropolitan Area (PSMA). Expressed relatively, one unit was added for every 4.5 units standing at the start of the period. In the city the ratio was one unit of new construction for every thirteen in the existing stock. The enormous suburban growth is seen in the addition of one unit for every 2.4 in existence in 1950. In the seven-year interval, four-fifths of the new residential construction in the metropolitan area took place outside of the city of Philadelphia.

Partly because of the desire of the postwar home purchaser for more spacious surroundings and partly because of the absorption of suitable building land within the city, Philadelphia's share of new construction in the metropolitan area has grown smaller in recent years. In 1950, one new unit was built in the city for every two built elsewhere in the metropolitan area; by 1956 the city's share of the total was but one in five. Philadelphia's large-scale urban renewal program, however, will tend to arrest if not reverse this trend.

Higher construction costs and increases in the size of units have resulted in rising prices for new dwellings. In 1950 the median price of a new house in the city was $9,300;[2] six years later the comparable figure was $13,000,[3] a rise of over 40 per cent. In fact, by 1956 it was exceedingly difficult to find a new home anywhere in the metropolitan area under $10,000 (only 3 per cent of total); almost 60 per cent were selling for $12,000 to $15,000.[4] On the other hand, relatively few very expensive houses were being built; only 5 per cent of the newly constructed homes, or 1,000 units, were priced at $20,000 or more. The new home market was thus dominated by the medium-priced home representing the intermediate ranges of size and quality.

New rental housing, never very enthusiastically received by more than a few Philadelphians, played a minor role in the postwar housing boom. Although there is some question about

[2] Philadelphia Housing Association.
[3] Derived from data supplied by the Bureau of Labor Statistics.
[4] Bureau of Labor Statistics.

the precise figure, the most liberal estimate places apartment construction in the metropolitan area slightly below 10 per cent of total residential building activity, while other data indicate that the proportion is closer to 5 per cent. For the nation as a whole, multiple dwellings accounted for only 15 per cent of total postwar residential construction. The Philadelphia area thus showed even less than this meager representation. Another factor is of particular interest. Fully one-third of all of the new rented units built in the metropolitan area since 1950 are single family homes. In view of the limited choice of new single family units for rent, the unorganized nature of this segment of the market, and the very high rents charged for most accommodations of this type, the proportion is astonishingly large. It indicates that there is a substantial segment of the population that seeks the advantages of a single family residence without assuming the obligations or the responsibilities of ownership.

THE MARKET FOR SINGLE FAMILY HOMES

Of the 600,000 households residing in Philadelphia at the end of 1956, 375,000 or approximately 62 per cent owned their homes compared with 56 per cent in 1950. In absolute terms, the number of owners increased by 46,000, while the number of renters declined by 31,000 during the six and three-quarter year interval.

If the increase in home ownership in the city was impressive, in the suburbs it was spectacular. From 1950 to 1956 the number of home owners in the suburbs grew by 180,000 at the same time that the rental sector of the market lost 10,000 families.[5] As a result, the rate of home ownership in the suburbs zoomed from 62 to 80 per cent during this short period.

[5] Although the terms "household" and "family," as defined by the U.S. Bureau of the Census, are not quite synonymous, they are occasionally used interchangeably in the text of this and succeeding chapters. In all tabular presentations and in all references to income, however, the precise wording is retained.

The proportion of renters and owners is not an accurate indication of the relative importance of the single family home versus the apartment unit. Almost 45 per cent of the renters in the city, and over 70 per cent of the renters in the suburbs, lived in one or two family structures. To put it another way, one and two family homes accounted for well over 75 per cent of the occupied housing stock in the city and 90 per cent in the suburban area.

The purchasers of existing as well as of new homes have sought and acquired dwellings in the middle price ranges. For the metropolitan area as a whole, 58 per cent of all home buyers in 1955 and 1956 found houses in the $10,000 to $20,000 price class and 13 per cent purchased homes that sold for $20,000 or more. Compared with the PSMA as a whole, Philadelphians tended to acquire less expensive houses. In Philadelphia, 53 per cent of the new or used homes purchased in 1955 and 1956 were priced under $10,000 and 45 per cent between $10,000 and $20,000. Less than 2 per cent were priced at $20,000 or more. In fact, only 4 per cent of all PSMA purchases in the most expensive price range were made in the city. Thus, in Philadelphia, it is quite obvious that moderately priced accommodations predominate, and the purchaser of an expensive home is far more inclined to look to the suburbs than to the city itself.

RENTAL HOUSING MARKET

In Philadelphia, households have tended to spend very little on rental housing. The quality of most of the rental accommodations is mediocre, and rent controls which continued until 1956 permitted rents to rise only moderately. But most important perhaps is the fact that as their incomes rise, Philadelphia renters tend to purchase single family homes. Throughout the metropolitan area more than three-quarters of the renter households pay a gross monthly rent of less than $80. Above this rent level, the distribution falls off sharply. Eighteen per cent of the renter households in the metropolitan area pay between $80 and $119 a month and less than 4 per cent occupy dwellings that rent for $120 or more. In the city the percentages are 12 and slightly more than 2, respectively. Approximately 44 per cent of all units renting for more than $80 per month in the metropolitan area are to be found in the counties outside of Philadelphia, despite the fact that the suburbs possess only one-third of the total number of rented dwelling units. (Appendix Tables I and II)

The data on recent renters display the same general patterns, but in a more sharply pronounced manner. For the entire metropolitan area, 22 per cent of the households whose tenure dates from 1955 or later are in the $80-$119 class, and slightly less than 4 per cent occupy units that rent for $120 or more. In the city the respective percentages are eleven and less than two, while in the suburban areas, 37 per cent of the renters chose units in the $80-$119 class and 7 per cent in the $120 and over group. Of most importance, 42 per cent of the recent renters in the metropolitan area selected units in the outlying counties, and over 70 per cent of the households that rented the more expensive dwellings (both the $80-$119 and over $120 class) were to be found in the suburban areas.

VACANCY RATES

Additions to the housing stock have eased the postwar housing shortage. For the past four or five years, the prices of existing houses have risen little in the city. At the same time, vacancy rates have moved upward, rising from 1.3 per cent in 1950 to 5.5 per cent in 1956. This rise is by no means an indication that an ample choice is available to all who seek places to live. The increase in empty housing units has been most marked in the low priced and low quality dwellings. Well-located and properly maintained units in the middle price-rent brackets are still in short supply, with vacancy rates of 1 to 2 per cent.

THE QUESTION OF THE CENTRAL CITY MARKET

In view of the nature of the postwar housing market in Philadelphia, one is inclined to raise many questions regarding the demand for the high priced, centrally located accommodation. What are the characteristics of such a market? What is its depth and who are the actual or potential clients? What are their preferences? How does demand vary as between the apartment unit and the single family home, the new versus the rehabilitated unit, the rented and the owned dwelling? Has a downtown market been in existence for some time, constituting an opportunity neglected by all but a handful of builders and sponsors?

Were these questions raised several years ago it would have been difficult if not impossible to mobilize sufficient evidence one way or another. But in recent years a body of data has been accumulated and the market for various types of accommodations has been tested. Briskly and consistently, single family units have been rehabilitated with some of them commanding prices that are substantial by virtually any standard. Many of the larger of these units have been subdivided into small apartments and have rented with celerity. More dramatic, perhaps, has been the very recent construction of several large and luxurious downtown apartment houses, a type of structure that had not been built in the center of the city for over a decade.

The following chapters report and analyze the characteristics of and recent trends in the central city housing market. Coupled with other data, they constitute the basis for the forecast of demand ventured in this study.

III

The Demand for High Rent Apartments in Central Philadelphia

Historically, the market for expensive apartments in central Philadelphia has been quite limited.[1] Philadelphia's families, steeped in the tradition of home ownership, have typically purchased a single family house as early in their careers as possible and, finances permitting, continued as home owners throughout their lives. Among well-to-do families few have preferred apartment living. This has certainly been true for the family with growing children; but it has also been true for the elderly couple whose space requirements are very moderate.

Philadelphians today still display a strong preference for homes of their own. The current rate of ownership among families earning over $5,000 exceeds 80 per cent.[2] Increasing progressively with the age of the head of the family, the ratio is in excess of 90 per cent for families in which the head of the household is over 55 years old. In the older group the 90 per cent ratio is found even among one and two person households who might be expected to welcome the convenience of a small apartment in view of the burdens of maintenance and repair faced by home owners.

Thus it is not surprising to find in Philadelphia today few apartments in the higher rent brackets. Of 226,000 occupied rental units in Philadelphia in 1956, fewer than 7,500 apartment units brought as much as $40 per room, the current mini-

---

[1] "Central Philadelphia," "center city," and "downtown" are used here synonymously to refer to the area between the two rivers and from Lombard to Spring Garden Streets.

[2] Except where otherwise noted, the information presented in this chapter is from unpublished special tabulations of the *1956 National Housing Inventory*, U.S. Bureau of the Census.

mum for almost all new center city apartments erected without government aid. In the entire metropolitan area, less than 10,000 units were to be found at this rent level.

The major concentration of the more expensive apartment construction is in downtown Philadelphia where there are now[3] approximately 3,000 high rent accommodations ($40 per room and up) in multiple structures. (Table I) The inventory of downtown luxury apartments is, moreover, soon to be expanded appreciably. As of January 1958, almost 1,400 new units were under construction,[4] 400 more were awaiting FHA approval, and an additional 200 were being brought up to new construction standards through renovation and repair. In the Society Hill redevelopment area itself, there are plans for more than 2,000 new and several hundred rehabilitated units. Without doubt other projects, as yet unannounced, will appear on the scene as the years pass. Thus downtown Philadelphia may, within the next ten or twelve years, witness the addition of perhaps as many as 5,000 units to its present inventory of high rent accommodations. This represents an average rate of expansion of 400 to 500 units a year, as contrasted with 200 per year since 1950.[5]

Where will the demand for these units come from? Will it be sufficient to absorb the market supply? To answer these and related questions several sources of demand are examined in the remaining sections of this chapter. First, the population composition is studied to determine the number of households that have the characteristics identified with the present clientele of the section of the housing market under consideration. Estimates are then made of the change that can be expected in the number of households with these characteristics, utilizing established local demographic trends. Consideration is then directed towards expected changes in aggregate future employment in

[3] December, 1957.

[4] Ambassador Towne House and Park Towne Place.

[5] From the late 1920's until 1950, the volume of construction at this quality level consisted almost entirely of 500 units built at 2601 Parkway in 1939.

Table I

INVENTORY OF APARTMENT UNITS BY RENTS PER
ROOM AND BY TYPE OF UNIT
CENTER CITY HIGH RENT APARTMENTS, 1957

Type of Dwelling Unit	Monthly Rent Per Room[a]		Per cent Distribution
	Minimum	Maximum	
Efficiency	$55	$75	30
One Bedroom	45	75	40
Two Bedrooms	45	70	20
Three Bedrooms and up	40	65[b]	10
TOTAL	—	—	100

[a] Excludes 2101 Co-operative and Rittenhouse Plaza due to problems of adjusting for down payments, tax remissions, and certain types of maintenance costs which are borne by the residents.
[b] Excludes a few large suites.
Source: Field survey.

the central district of Philadelphia and in other sections of the metropolitan area.

In order to take account of increments in demand that will arise because of expected increases in the higher income groups in the population, projections are made of the way in which anticipated shifts in real per capita income will influence Philadelphia's income distribution. Special attention is then paid to the extent to which the central city will be able to compete with other sections of Philadelphia and its environs, particularly for the group in the population that possesses all the characteristics of the complete urbanite.

In addition to the evaluation of these demand factors, consideration is given to anticipated changes in the present housing supply. With the passage of time, some units presently in the high rent class will gradually decline in quality because of age and obsolescence. The number of units that will seep into lower rent categories will be contingent upon maintenance policies, preference shifts, and the volume, quality, and location of new construction. The probable effects of these factors are examined and quantified.

The sum total of all of these factors, with due allowance for vacancies and for the accumulated backlog of demand, represents the extent to which luxury housing in central Philadelphia can be absorbed between 1958 and 1970, the maximum period within which the construction contemplated in the Society Hill area will take place.

The primary data required for the projections of demand both for apartment and single family structures were drawn from several sources. The current inventory and occupancy rates of high quality downtown apartments and single family residences were established by a field survey of the entire central area. The characteristics of the present residents of these structures were identified by personal interviews with a 4 per cent sample of apartment occupants and a 20 per cent sample of residents of rehabilitated single family homes.[6]

Additional data on downtown residents were obtained by a special tabulation of questionnaires administered to center city residents by the Bureau of the Census in connection with its *National Housing Inventory* (*NHI*) of December 1956. The NHI tabulations were also the major source of information on all households in the PSMA. These tabulations provided the basis for comparisons between downtown demanders and the larger population, as well as bench-mark data for the projections to 1970. The final source of primary data was a survey of approximately sixty residents of high quality apartments in the outlying sections of Philadelphia. The data obtained in this

[6] Approximately one-half of the interviews were conducted in the summer of 1957 as part of a special study by the American Council to Improve Our Neighborhoods and *Fortune* magazine. These organizations very graciously consented to make the schedules available to the Institute for Urban Studies for this research project.

field investigation were not, however, utilized formally in the estimation procedures.

CENTRAL CITY APARTMENT RESIDENTS

Profile of Characteristics: The households that occupy downtown apartments constitute a readily distinguishable group; in fact, there are remarkably few deviations from the group pattern.

The household interviews revealed the following characteristics: 98 per cent of the heads of households were over 35 years old; in 94 per cent of the cases there were no children in the household; 96 per cent enjoyed a family income of more than $5,000 a year; 90 per cent either worked in center city, or were not in the labor force. (Table II) Over 80 per cent of the respondents fit into all four categories. Over 90 per cent fit into the first three categories. Every respondent had at least one of the four characteristics.

By comparison, in the total metropolitan area, less than 80 per cent of the household heads are over 35; only 49 per cent have annual family incomes of more than $5,000; 50 per cent have no children; and 32 per cent work in center city or do not work. Only 6 per cent, or 68,000 households, fit into all four categories. Thus, center city housing draws from a relatively small segment of the population, and has attracted an extremely small proportion (less than 5 per cent) of that segment.[7]

[7] Interestingly, similar household characteristics are found among residents of luxury apartments in Manhattan. In the high rent apartments under rent control, almost 95 per cent of the household heads are over 35 years of age and almost 90 per cent of the families have incomes over *$10,000* a year. Only 63 per cent of the households are childless, however, and only one-half consist of one or two persons (excluding servants). No data were gathered on employment location. The greater affluence of the downtown New York resident is reflected in the fact that 97 per cent of the apartment rents are above $200 a month. Compared with its Philadelphia counterpart, the New York family is larger and tends to occupy larger apartments. Ninety-five per cent of the high rent accommodations in New York have four or more rooms. See Morton Schussheim, *High Rent Housing and Rent Control in New York City* (New York: Temporary State Housing Rent Commission, April 1958), Chapter 6 and Appendix tables.

Table II

SELECTED HOUSEHOLD CHARACTERISTICS OF RESI-
DENTS OF HIGH RENT CENTER CITY APARTMENTS
COMPARED WITH ALL HOUSEHOLDS
PHILADELPHIA STANDARD METROPOLITAN AREA, 1957

Characteristics	Center City	PSMA
One and Two Persons Households	87.2	36.7
Head of Household over 35 years old	97.8	77.8
Female Head of Household	38.6	16.1
Household without Children	94.1	49.6
Family Income over $5,000	96.1	48.9
Family Income over $10,000	50.4	9.9
Head of Household in Professional or Managerial Position	57.8	19.6
Head of Household Employed in Center City	66.5	13.6
Head of Household Unemployed or not in Labor Force	23.5	18.5

Source: *1956 National Housing Inventory*, U.S. Bureau of the Census, unpublished data; and field surveys of center city high rent apartments, 1957.

Several other contrasts could be presented, but two more will suffice. The small household accounted for virtually all respondents, with one and two-person groups comprising 87 per cent of total and three-person households, 12 per cent.[8] Households with more than three persons were found in less than 1 per cent of the cases. These figures contrast very sharply with the PSMA where one and two-person households are 37 per cent of the total; three persons, 21 per cent; and more than three, 42 per cent.

The downtown apartment dwellers tended to concentrate in

[8] Contrary to widespread opinion, very few households consisted of two or more *unrelated* individuals. The absence of such households stems partly from management policy and partly from the preference of younger persons for cheaper accommodations in order to hold housing expenditures at a minimum. See Chapter V.

professional, technical, and managerial occupations with three out of five household heads in positions of this type. The second largest group, 26 per cent, consisted of elderly persons and younger individuals with independent incomes. Only 13 per cent held clerical or sales jobs and none were operatives or laborers. In contrast, in the PSMA, 20 per cent held professional or managerial jobs, 11 per cent were clerical or sales personnel, and 18 per cent were operatives or laborers. Although the proportion of individuals in the PSMA who were not employed (27 per cent) differed little from the ratio in central city, in the larger area the group consisted of the unemployed as well as pensioners and rentiers. (Appendix Table III)

Tendency Ratios: The profile of apartment residents, while interesting in itself as a description of the urban type, serves the more important purpose of providing the analyst with an index of the sources of demand for downtown apartments. These sources are brought into sharper focus when the various demographic and employment characteristics described individually in the preceding paragraphs are consolidated in a single table or matrix. This has been done in Table III, which presents a distribution of the 3,000 residents in our demand group according to their income, family type, and age and employment characteristics of the head.[9] The population cells which account for the largest segment of downtown demand have been grouped in the upper left hand corner of the table.

According to these data almost 40 per cent of the demand comes from workers in the 45-64 age group employed in center city. Retired families over 65 constitute the next largest segment comprising, however, less than one-sixth of the total. At the other end of the scale, the four-way distribution of family characteristics reveals that within the highly potential group, virtually no demand comes from household heads in the 35-44 bracket who are not employed.

[9] These figures are estimates based upon the sample of households and are therefore subject to sampling variations. The reader should be cautioned that the percentage error tends to be large in the smaller cells.

Table III

NUMBER OF HOUSEHOLDS BY FAMILY TYPE, AGE OF HEAD, FAMILY INCOME, AND EMPLOYMENT LOCATION, PHILADELPHIA CENTER CITY HIGH RENT APARTMENTS, 1957

| Income and Place of Employment | Families Without Children | | | | Families with Children Total* | Total |
| | Age of Head of Household | | | | | |
	65+	45-64	35-44	Under 35		
$5,000-$9,999						
Works in Center City	230	440	170	20	60	920
Not Employed	240	100	0	0	40	380
$10,000 and over						
Works in Center City	150	700	130	10	10	1,000
Not Employed	200	120	0	0	0	320
$5,000 and over						
Works Elsewhere Than Center City	40	60	50	40	50	240
Under $5,000						
Total	110	20	0	0	10	140
TOTAL	970	1,440	350	70	170	3,000

* None under 35; none 65 or over.

Variations in the contribution of various population groups in the PSMA to the center city market, as shown in Table III, are associated not only with the characteristics, but also with the size of the population group. Thus it is not evident from Table III whether the extremely small proportion of demanders under 35 years of age, for example, relates to the preferences of this group, or their numbers in the total population or both. In order to examine the propensity or tendency of various types of households to choose center city as a place of residence, a matrix identical to that for center city was constructed for the entire PSMA household population. (Table IV) This table reveals the size or total potential of each population group, or cell, in the PSMA. It is at once obvious that most of center city

Table IV

NUMBER OF HOUSEHOLDS BY FAMILY TYPE, AGE OF HEAD, FAMILY INCOME, AND EMPLOYMENT LOCATION, PHILADELPHIA STANDARD METROPOLITAN AREA, 1957

| Income and Place of Employment | Families Without Children | | | | Families With Children Total | Total |
| | Age of Head of Household | | | | | |
	65+	45-64	35-44	Under 35		
$5,000-$9,999						
Works in Center City	2,110	22,190	4,900	4,220	40,620	74,040
Does Not Work	12,580	8,220	660	1,000	19,160	41,620
$10,000 and up						
Works in Center City	1,590	7,840	840	610	12,800	23,680
Does Not Work	6,840	1,460	330	0	1,020	9,650
$5,000 and up						
Works Elsewhere Than Center City	14,280	112,260	31,490	24,530	282,550	465,110
Under $5,000						
Total	129,500	145,630	31,280	31,740	250,350	588,500
TOTAL	166,900	297,600	69,500	62,100	606,500	1,202,600

demand comes from groups which account for but a small proportion of total PSMA population, and that with few exceptions the family types that show the least preference for center city residence are indeed the most numerous. For example, households with children and with earnings of less than $5,000 a year constitute 21 per cent of the PSMA households, but less than 1 per cent of the downtown apartment demanders. Similarly, households, whose annual incomes are $5,000 or over and in which the principal wage earner is employed outside of the central district, represent 39 per cent of the PSMA, and only 8 per cent of the central city apartment dwellers.

Table V

PER CENT OF HOUSEHOLDS IN PHILADELPHIA
STANDARD METROPOLITAN AREA LIVING IN
CENTER CITY APARTMENTS BY FAMILY TYPE,
AGE OF HEAD, FAMILY INCOME, AND
EMPLOYMENT LOCATION, 1957

Income and Place of Employment	Families Without Children				Families with Children	Total
	Age of Head of Household					
	65	45-64	35-44	Under 35		
$5,000-$9,999						
Works in Center City	10.9	2.0	3.5	0.5	0.2	1.2
Does Not Work	1.9	1.2	0	0	0.2	0.9
$10,000 and up						
Works in Center City	9.4	8.9	15.5	1.6	0.1	4.2
Does Not Work	2.9	8.2	0	0	0	3.3
$5,000 and up						
Works Elsewhere Than Center City	0.3	*	0.3	0.2	*	*
Under $5,000						
Total	0.1	*	0	0	*	*
TOTAL	0.6	0.5	0.5	0.1	*	0.2

* Less than one-tenth of 1 per cent.

If each cell in the center city matrix is divided by its counterpart in the PSMA matrix, the quotients represent the proportion of potential demand which center city is currently able to realize from the various population groups. The results of these calculations are presented in Table V. This matrix restates and quantifies observations that have already been encountered. It shows that:

(1) The central city apartment demanders constitute an extremely small proportion (0.25 per cent) of all PSMA households.

(2) Downtown Philadelphia does not attract a very large proportion of any particular population group in the metropolitan area. The largest representation is to be found among childless households where the head is 35 to 44, earns in excess of $10,000 a year, and is employed in center city. Approximately one-sixth of the PSMA families with these characteristics are to be found in center city.

(3) There is a great range of variation in the tendency ratios. Seven of the thirty cells have no representative in central city apartments, and in twelve cells the ratio is less than 1 per cent. The remaining ratios are scattered: six cells have tendency ratios of 1.0-3.9; three cells are in the 7.0-9.9 range; and two exceed 10.0.

The ten cells in the PSMA matrix, from which 2,400 out of 3,000 current downtown apartment demanders are drawn, contain in aggregate 68,000 households. Thus, of the group that possesses the attributes that characterize downtown housing demanders, 97 per cent have chosen to live elsewhere.[10] The largest segment of demand lost to center city by the competition of supply elsewhere is accounted for by home owners. Since home ownership involves a different type of dwelling accommodation, a new matrix was prepared that shows the

---

[10] A discussion of the likelihood of drawing this group into the ranks of central city apartment demanders appears in a later section of this chapter.

tendency of families to live in center city once they have decided to become renters instead of home owners. (Table VIII)[11]

Table VI

NUMBER OF RENTER HOUSEHOLDS BY FAMILY TYPE, AGE OF HEAD, FAMILY INCOME, AND EMPLOYMENT LOCATION, PHILADELPHIA STANDARD METROPOLITAN AREA, 1957

| Income and Place of Employment | Families Without Children | | | | | Families with Children Total | Total |
| | Age of Head of Household | | | | | |
	65+	45-64	35-44	Under 35	Total		
$5,000-$9,999							
Works in Center City	740	4,355	2,325	1,455	6,755		15,630
Does Not Work	1,385	2,300	600	950	1,590		6,825
$10,000 and up							
Works in Center City	170	830	585	15	465		2,065
Does Not Work	230	145	10	0	180		565
$5,000 and up							
Works Elsewhere Than Center City	2,970	16,625	9,730	10,510	45,995		85,830
Under $5,000							
Total	32,670	50,670	18,870	24,375	109,500		236,085
TOTAL	38,165	74,925	32,120	37,305	164,485		347,000

Of the renter group in the ten cells with the highest potential for the center city, the downtown area currently captures approximately 17 per cent of potential demand. Among middle-aged and elderly renters with incomes over $10,000, more

[11] Two tables (VI and VII) present background data on the number and proportion of renter to total households in the PSMA.

Table VII

RENTER HOUSEHOLDS AS A PER CENT OF ALL
HOUSEHOLDS IN PHILADELPHIA STANDARD
METROPOLITAN AREA, BY FAMILY TYPE,
AGE OF HEAD, FAMILY INCOME, AND
EMPLOYMENT LOCATION, 1957

Income and Place of Employment	Families Without Children				Families with Children Total	Total
	\t 65+	45-64	35-44	Under 35		
	Age of Head of Household					
$5,000-$9,999						
Works in Center City	35	20	47	35	17	21
Not Employed	11	28	87	95	8	16
$10,000 and up						
Works in Center City	11	11	70	3	4	9
Not Employed	3	10	3	0	18	6
Over $5,000						
Works Elsewhere Than Center City	21	15	31	43	16	19
Under $5,000						
Total	25	35	60	77	44	40
TOTAL	23	25	46	60	27	29

than four-fifths prefer center city to other locations in the
Philadelphia area, and, for some of these family types, the
ratio approaches 90 per cent.

It is of special interest to point up the contrast between this
group and the residents of similar apartment houses located in
outlying sections of the city. The outlying structures are of
equal quality but somewhat lower in rent ($35 per room as
against $40 for downtown units) by virtue of their greater dis-
tance from center city. While the occupants of these units tend

Table VIII

PER CENT OF RENTER HOUSEHOLDS IN PHILADELPHIA
STANDARD METROPOLITAN AREA LIVING IN CENTER
CITY APARTMENTS BY FAMILY TYPE, AGE OF HEAD,
FAMILY INCOME, AND EMPLOYMENT LOCATION, 1957

| Income and Place of Employment | Families Without Children | | | | Families with Children Total | Total |
| | Age of Head of Household | | | | | |
	65+	45-64	35-44	Under 35		
$5,000-$9,999						
Works in Center City	31	10	7	1	1	6
Not Employed	17	4	0	0	3	
$10,000 and up						
Works in Center City	88	84	22	67	2	49
Not Employed	87	83	0	0	0	57
$5,000 and up						
Works Elsewhere Than Center City	1	(*a*)	(*a*)	(*a*)	(*a*)	(*a*)
Under $5,000						
Total	(*a*)	(*b*)	0	0	(*b*)	(*b*)
TOTAL	3	2	1	0.2	0.1	1

a Less than one-half of 1 per cent.
b Less than one-tenth of 1 per cent.

to have the same family type, age, and occupational characteristics, on the average they have lower incomes and a much smaller proportion work in center city. It would thus appear that for childless renter families the combined effect of these two factors weighs heavily in the choice between a downtown and an outlying location.

Population and Household Growth: At this point there is little doubt that the demand for centrally located housing is drawn from an atypical sector of the total population. How will this sector change during the period in which new construction in Society Hill will be placed on the market? The aggregate number of households in the Philadelphia Standard Metropolitan Area is expected to increase by approximately 174,000 between 1957 and 1970, bringing the total to 1,376,900 thirteen years hence.[12] (Table IX) This increase of

Table IX

PROJECTED NUMBER OF HOUSEHOLDS BY AGE OF HEAD, PHILADELPHIA STANDARD METROPOLITAN AREA, 1957-1970

Age of Head	Number of Households		Change 1957-1970	
	1957	1970	Number	Per cent
Under 25	32,500	56,700	24,200	74.5
25-34	234,600	241,600	7,000	3.0
35-44	298,100	293,200	−4,900	−1.6
45-64	457,200	575,000	117,800	25.8
65 and up	180,200	210,400	30,200	16.8
TOTAL	1,202,600	1,376,900	174,300	14.5

approximately 14 per cent will be much greater for some age groups than for others. The number of household heads under 25, for example, will rise by almost 75 per cent while in the

[12] This estimate is based upon a population projection made by the Philadelphia City Planning Commission. The population figures were translated into households by calculating the percentage of persons in each age-sex group, or "cell," of the population that tend to become heads of households and applying these percentages to the 1970 population distributions. This technique, known as the "age specific headship ratio" method, is described in detail in another study. See Louis Winnick, *American Housing and Its Use* (New York: John Wiley & Sons, Inc., 1957); also Ned Shilling "Net Household Formation. A Demographic Analysis" (unpublished Master's Thesis, Faculty of Political Science, Columbia University, 1954).

age group 35-44 an absolute decline appears likely to occur. Since center city draws its demanders almost exclusively from persons over 35 years of age, the percentage increase of groups that are potential to the downtown market will be somewhat different from that for the entire Philadelphia Standard Metropolitan Area. The amount of the difference can be determined by relating the projected increase in each age group to the relative importance of that group in the center city market. This calculation (Table X) shows the increment in the downtown potential to be in the neighborhood of 20 per cent, a considerably larger figure than that for the total PSMA market.

Table X

IMPACT OF INCREASE OF HOUSEHOLDS IN
PHILADELPHIA STANDARD METROPOLITAN
AREA FROM 1957 TO 1970 ON CENTER CITY
DEMAND FOR HIGH RENT APARTMENTS
DURING THE SAME PERIOD

Age of Head	Distribution of Center City High Rent Households 1957	Projected Increase 1957-1970	Weighted Projected Increase 1957-1970 (Col. 1 times Col. 2)
	Per cent	*Per cent*	*Per cent*
Under 25	0	74.5	0
25-34	2.2	3.0	+0.1
35-44	12.4	−1.6	−0.2
45-64	53.0	25.8	+13.9
65 and up	32.4	16.8	+5.4
TOTAL	100.0	.....	+19.2

Note: The 19.2 per cent increase calculated above could also be obtained by multiplying the populations of each of the 1957 and 1970 age cells in Table IX by the percentage of the cell living in center city in 1957 and then subtracting the 1957 products from the 1970 products.

In other words, on the basis of anticipated increases in the number of households of the types that have exhibited a preference for high quality apartments and a downtown environment, the market for units in the upper rent ranges in center city will expand from 3,000 in 1957 to approximately 3,600 families by 1970. This estimate is a first approximation that does not take into account employment changes, income increases, or the various other determinants of new construction.

SHIFTS IN EMPLOYMENT PATTERNS

An unusually large proportion of the occupants of the high rent central city apartments either live within a very short distance of their place of employment or are not limited in the selection of a residential location by job considerations. Two-thirds work in the central business district (CBD) itself, and 23 per cent are not in the labor force. Only 10 per cent, compared with over 80 per cent of all employed household heads in the metropolitan area, work outside the central area of the city.

It was brought out quite clearly in the interviews with the downtown families that convenience to job was a major factor in the locational choice of those who were employed and that proximity to downtown activities was of prime importance to those who did not work. Without doubt, center city will continue to appeal primarily to the same two groups of families. It is clear, therefore, that the downtown market will be considerably influenced by employment opportunities in the CBD and by the extent to which there is growth in the retired sector of the population.

According to various published estimates, the rate of employment growth in the CBD is expected to be moderate at best, and, in any event, much lower than the average for the PSMA. As a consequence there will be a severe reduction in the volume of demand resulting from any overall rise in the number of households who are otherwise favorably disposed to the idea of downtown living. A greater than average addition to the number of retired households will, however, partially offset this factor. The net effect of changes in employment patterns between now and 1970 will be to reduce the previous approximation of a 20 per cent increase in demand by a range of one-third to two-thirds. A description of the assumptions and calculations on which these estimates are based are presented in the paragraphs below.

Employment Growth in Center City: The increase in population and employment in the Philadelphia area over the coming years will be accompanied by internal changes in the urban structure that will favor growth in some sections and inhibit expansion elsewhere. One of the most important internal shifts of the recent past, and one which is expected to continue, is the relative decline of centrally located industrial, commercial, and, to a lesser extent, professional employment in conjunction with the rapid urbanization of outlying sections of the PSMA. Since World War II, new job opportunities in outlying areas have increased very rapidly. These have preceded, or accompanied or followed, suburban residential growth; but in virtually all cases they have increased much faster than the number of jobs in the more inlying sections, including center city itself. Since 1950, the metropolitan area has gained more than 200,000 workers while the central business district, which provides employment for between 20 and 25 per cent of the entire labor force in the PSMA, has remained relatively stable.[13] If employment in center city continues at its present general level while the principal job expansion occurs in other

[13] In fact, fragmentary data of the Urban Traffic and Transportation Board suggest that total employment in the CBD has stayed at roughly the same magnitude since 1947. For an estimate of metropolitan area and CBD employment changes from 1950 to 1955, see *Transportation Requirements—Population and Employment* (Technical Memorandum No. 3) prepared by Marketers' Research Service, Inc. for the City of Philadelphia Urban Traffic and Transportation Board (1955), Table 21, p. 144. See also the reports of the Pennsylvania State Employment Service.

sections, a sizeable share of the potential market for new downtown residential construction will be lost to other areas.

The future of employment in the central business district has received considerable attention from local public agencies and business groups, and a number of projections have been made. The most optimistic forecast for the central area shows a 19 per cent gain during the period 1950 to 1980.[14] A more conservative estimate suggests an 8 per cent rise from 1955 to 1980.[15] At the bottom of the scale, some analysts feel that both estimates are too high and that the absence of growth in CBD employment for more than ten years is indicative of the future trend of the area. Thus, the estimates range from about 0.6 per cent per year down to zero. For the thirteen-year period, 1957 to 1970, this projected range of rates of growth yields an estimated increase in central city employment of zero to 8 per cent.[16]

These estimates must be adjusted for anticipated changes in the occupational distribution of employment in center city. Declines in manufacturing, retailing, and wholesaling and increases in consumer and business services are expected.[17] These shifts, if they do come to pass, will reduce the number of blue collar jobs and at the same time increase white collar employment in the higher income brackets. Thus, even if center city shows no increase in total employment, there may be some accretion in the number of job opportunities for our demand group.

The amount of this increase is difficult to estimate because of lack of adequate employment data. A rough approximation may be obtained, however, if projected growth in non-manu-

[14] *Pilot Plan, A Study for the Comprehensive Plan* (Philadelphia: Philadelphia City Planning Commission, February 1957), Table I, p. 58.

[15] See Howard Lapin, "Transportation Analysis in Philadelphia Metropolitan Region," *Papers and Proceedings*, Regional Science Association (1957), Volume III, p. 205.

[16] This calculation assumes that the projected growth rates to 1980 can be applied with a fair degree of accuracy to the shorter period.

[17] *Pilot Plan, op. cit.*, p. 59.

facturing activity is used as an indicator of the likely expansion in the occupational and income categories that feed the down-town high rent market. According to the optimistic forecast for total central area employment, cited above, non-manufac-turing employment in center city is expected to rise by 24 per cent during the period 1950 to 1980.[18] This is equivalent to an increase of about 10 per cent for the 1957-1970 interval. The upper limit of the estimated range of increase was therefore raised from 8 per cent to 10 per cent.

Table XI

INCREASE OF NONWORKING HOUSEHOLD HEADS
PHILADELPHIA STANDARD METROPOLITAN AREA
1957-1970
(Thousands of Persons)

Age of Head	Nonworking Household Heads 1957		Nonworking Household Heads 1970		Per cent Increase 1957-1970	
	Income Under $5,000	Income $5,000 & Over	Income Under $5,000	Income $5,000 & Over	Income Under $5,000	Income $5,000 & Over
Under 25	3.0	0	5.3	0	76.7	0
25-34	11.2	0.1	11.5	0.1	2.7	0
35-44	15.5	1.2	15.2	1.2	1.9	0
45-64	57.2	3.0	71.9	3.8	25.7	26.7
65 Plus	126.9	3.7	148.1	4.3	16.7	16.2
	213.8	8.0	252.0	9.4	17.9	17.5

Increase in "Non-employed" Household Heads: The poten-tial demand for center city apartments will, as noted earlier, be augmented by an increase in the number of retired workers and widows who currently constitute almost one-quarter of the downtown high rent housing market. Among non-employed

[18] *Ibid.*

household heads having family incomes in excess of $5,000 annually, the increment in demand for downtown apartments will be in the neighborhood of 20 per cent.

The estimate of the expansion of this sector of the market required three steps. First, "non-employment" rates, by income and age of head, were derived for the PSMA for the year 1956

Table XII

IMPACT OF INCREASE OF NONWORKING HOUSEHOLD HEADS IN PHILADELPHIA STANDARD METROPOLITAN AREA ON DEMAND FOR CENTER CITY HIGH RENT APARTMENTS, 1957-1970

Income and Age of Non-employed Heads	Distribution of Nonworking Residents of Center City Apartments 1957	Projected Increase 1957-1970	Weighted Projected Increase 1957-1970
	Per cent	Per cent	Per cent
Income $5,000 & Over			
Under 44	0	0	0
45-64	36.5	26.7	10.5
65 plus	60.4	16.2	9.7
Income Under $5,000			
All Ages	3.1	17.9	0.5
TOTAL	100	....	20.7

from tabulations of the *National Housing Inventory*. (Tables XI and XII) These rates were then applied to the estimated age-income distribution of households in 1970 in order to obtain the absolute and percentage increase of non-working heads that could be expected in the metropolitan area by that date. Finally, the percentage increases for each category of nonworking heads for the PSMA were weighed according to the importance of that category in the aggregate demand for center city high rental apartments in 1957. (Table XII) No account was taken of the possible impact on the market stemming from a trend toward earlier retirement.

Increase of Other Employment: Approximately 10 per cent of demand for downtown apartments stems from household heads holding jobs outside the central business district. Expansion of this segment of the employment market was calculated by subtracting from the total number of household heads in 1970 those working in center city and those not working at all. Using this procedure, it was determined that the residual group would show an increase of roughly 16 to 18 per cent, corresponding to the upper and lower range of the projected employment figures for center city. (Table XIII)

Table XIII

PROJECTED INCREASE IN HOUSEHOLDS BY EMPLOY-
MENT LOCATION OF THE HEAD, ASSUMING TWO
DIFFERENT GROWTH RATES FOR CENTRAL
BUSINESS DISTRICT, PHILADELPHIA STANDARD
METROPOLITAN AREA, 1957-1970
(thousands of households)

Employment Location of Head	Households 1957	Assumption I Stable Employment in CBD		Assumption II 10 Per cent Employment Increase in CBD	
		Households 1970	Per cent Increase 1957-1970	Households 1970	Per cent Increase 1957-1970
Works in CBD	165.4	165.4	0	181.9	10.0
Works Elsewhere in PSMA	815.4	950.1	16.8	933.6	14.5
Does Not Work	221.8	261.4	17.9	261.4	17.9
TOTAL	1,202.6	1,376.9	14.5	1,376.9	14.5

Impact of Employment Changes on Center City Market:
When the projected increases in the three groups above are
weighed according to their importance in the downtown rental
market in 1957, the impact of the shifting employment patterns
on demand can be gauged. (Table XIV) If jobs in the CBD

Table XIV

IMPACT OF EMPLOYMENT GROWTH AND REDISTRIBU-
TION IN PHILADELPHIA STANDARD METROPOLITAN
AREA ON DEMAND FOR CENTER CITY HIGH RENT
APARTMENTS, ASSUMING TWO DIFFERENT GROWTH
RATES FOR CENTRAL BUSINESS DISTRICT, 1957-1970

Employment Location of Head	Distribution of Center City High Rent Households 1957	Assumption I Stable Employment in CBD		Assumption II 10 Per cent Employment Growth in CBD	
		Projected Increase 1957-1970	Weighted Projected Increase 1957-1970	Projected Increase 1957-1970	Weighted Projected Increase 1957-1970
Works in CBD	66.5	0	0	10.0	6.7
Works Elsewhere in PSMA	10.0	16.8	1.7	14.5	1.5
Does Not Work	23.5	20.7	4.8	20.7	4.8
	100.0	...	6.5	...	13.0

remain at the same level from 1957 through 1970, demand for
center city apartments may be expected to expand by only 6.5
per cent, and even if the downtown area realized the maximum
employment growth (10 per cent) that any analyst has projected
for it, the increase in apartment demand associated with this
expansion will not exceed 13 per cent. In other words, only one-
third to two-thirds of the previously computed 20 per cent increase in households potential to center city living may be ex-

Table XV

REAL INCOME TRENDS IN THE UNITED STATES, 1929-1955

	Per Capita Income Before Taxes[a]		Average Personal Income Per Family Before Taxes[b]		Average Personal Income Per Family After Taxes[b]		Average Personal Income Per Household Before Taxes[c]		Average Personal Income Per Household After Taxes[c]	
	Total (1956 $)	Annual Rate of Increase to 1955 (%)	Total (1955 $)	Annual Rate of Increase to 1955 (%)	Total (1955 $)	Annual Rate of Increase to 1955 (%)	Total (1950 $)	Annual Rate of Increase to 1953 (%)	Total (1950 $)	Annual Rate of Increase to 1953 (%)
1929	1,081	1.66	3,760	1.48	3,730	1.12	—	—	—	—
1930	984	2.11	—	—	—	—	3,650	1.17	3,780	1.63
1933	765	3.58	3,318	2.58	—	—	—	—	—	—
1935	907	3.06	—	—	—	—	—	—	—	—
1940	1,118	2.66	—	—	—	—	3,830	1.70	3,960	2.53
1945	1,624	.24	—	—	—	—	—	—	—	—
1947	1,427	1.69	4,870	1.57	4,380	1.62	4,600	.61	5,190	.91
1950	1,536	1.56	4,940	2.24	4,520	1.95	4,730	.28	5,210	1.69
1952	1,548	1.76	5,240	1.75	4,680	2.09	4,710	1.27	5,410	.28
1953	1,592	2.11	5,430	.82	4,840	1.31	4,770	—	5,480	—
1955	1,660	—	5,520	—	4,980	—	—	—	—	—

[a] *Historical and Descriptive Supplement to Economic Indicators, 1957* (prepared for the Joint Economic Committee by the Committee Staff and the Office of Statistical Standards, Bureau of the Budget [United States Government Printing Office, Washington, 1957]).

[b] *Income & Housing* (Staff Report to the Subcommittee on Housing of the Committee on Banking and Currency, United States Senate [United States Government Printing Office, Washington, 1957]), p. 83.

[c] Dewhurst and Associates, *America's Needs and Resources, a New Survey* (New York: The Twentieth Century Fund, 1955), Table XXX, p. 89.

pected to be absorbed by our market. The previously estimated demand of 3,600 high rent units in 1970 is, therefore, reduced to a range of 3,200 to 3,400.

ANTICIPATED INCOME GROWTH AND DISTRIBUTION

Housing demand in the past three decades has been buttressed by substantial growth in income and by its wider distribution. Per capita real income is now more than 50 per cent above the level achieved during the full employment year of 1929. (Table XV) The increase in the lowest quintile of the income distribution has been several times that in the upper fifth. Moreover, the relatively greater rise in the lower income groups has continued to the most recent year (1954) for which data are available. (Tables XVI and XVII)

Table XVI

TREND OF REAL INCOME FOR NONFARM FAMILIES,
SHOWING PERCENTAGE INCREASES OVER 1947
FOR MEDIANS OF EACH FIFTH, 1950-1954

	(Per cent)				
Medians	1950	1951	1952	1953	1954
Lowest fifth	1.9	13.4	17.1	25.6	22.2
Second fifth	3.4	8.2	14.2	20.2	17.8
Middle fifth	4.6	8.3	12.8	18.3	16.1
Fourth fifth	3.3	5.6	10.5	15.4	13.3
Highest fifth	1.8	0.5	2.0	2.9	1.6

Source: *Income and Housing, op. cit.*, Table V, p. 82. Original data from Department of Commerce.

The impact of the changing income pattern on the housing market was arrested by the depression of the thirties and by World War II when only defense construction was permitted

Table XVII

AVERAGE INCOMES OF FARM AND NONFARM FAMILIES, 1935-36 AND 1954, AND PER CENT INCREASES

| | Average Incomes (1955 dollars) | | Per cent Increase |
	1935-36	1954	1935-36 to 1954
Lowest fifth	759	1,315	73
Second fifth	1,691	3,061	81
Third fifth	2,578	4,451	73
Fourth fifth	3,780	5,985	58
Highest fifth	9,336	11,952	28

Source: *Income and Housing, op. cit.,* Table VI, p. 82. Original data from Department of Commerce.

to take place. In the last decade, however, the pressure of demand has been released. New construction has exceeded household formation by a considerable margin, resulting in the rapid abandonment of the lower quality sectors of the housing stock. In Philadelphia, for example, although the population has remained virtually constant since 1950, over 50,000 new dwelling units have been built and almost 20 per cent of the substandard stock has been vacated. Continued increase in real incomes is to be expected, and this will materially benefit the more expensive sectors of the rental market, even though on balance it may increase the rate of home ownership in the community as a whole.

The derivation of quantitative estimates of future income distributions and their effects upon housing demand requires three steps. First, a rate of growth consistent with past trends and future potentialities must be chosen. Second, the aggregate increase must be distributed among the various income classes. Third, after the income increments for each class interval have been calculated, their effect on the housing market must be adjudged.

Rate of Growth in Real Income: The best available guide to future trends in our standard of living is the record of improvements in material welfare over past years. The historical rate of growth in real income (Table XV), however, has varied widely between any two years and also depends, in considerable measure, upon whose income is being examined. For this study, the average annual rate of increase between 1929 and 1955 was selected for projection into the near future, primarily because full employment prevailed in the initial and terminal years.[19]

For the 1929 to 1955 period, there are several measures of the growth of real income. For example, the income of families and individuals increased at an average rate of 1.5 per cent per year before taxes, and at a rate of 1.0 per cent after taxes. Per capita income after taxes rose by 1.7 per cent annually. Of these three measures, the first is most closely associated with housing demand, and the rate itself is consistent with estimates of future income trends.[20] Expanded at this rate, the projected increase in real income between 1957 and 1970 amounts to approximately 20 per cent.

Changes in Income Distribution: Before the estimated income increase can be applied to the income distribution of the population, some assumptions must be made regarding the apportionment of the increment among various income groups.

[19] In contrast, the trend from 1935 to 1955 reflects both gains in productivity and gains due to an increase in the employment of resources. The 1929 to 1955 period has the additional advantage of being long enough to give some assurance that temporary aberrations have not unduly biased the data. It should be pointed out, however, that the trend for the period as a whole was influenced considerably by more than a decade of war and depression.

[20] See *Income and Housing* (staff report to the Subcommittee on Housing of the Committee on Banking and Currency, United States Senate, [United States Government Printing Office, Washington, 1957]), p. 75, for a discussion of available series of income projections. Also Gerhard Colm, Theodore Geiger, and Manuel Helzner, *The Economy of the American People* (National Planning Association, Washington, D.C., 1958, Appendix Table 15, pp. 162-63. Also, *Economic Growth in the United States, Its Past and Future* (Committee for Economic Development, February 1958), p. 43.

The demand for high rent housing comes almost entirely from families that earn more than $5,000. If most of the increase in real income should redound to the benefit of those families now earning less than $5,000, the effect on the market would be much different than if it were to be allocated proportionately among all families.

If the trends in the distribution of income over the past thirty years were projected, families in the lower income brackets would be allocated greater percentage income increases than those in the upper levels. It is evident, however, that this trend cannot continue indefinitely, and in fact the tendency towards equalization has slowed down in the past few years. (Table XVIII)[21]

Table XVIII

PER CENT OF AGGREGATE WAGE OR SALARY INCOME
RECEIVED BY EACH FIFTH OF WAGE OR SALARY
RECIPIENTS RANKED BY INCOME, 1939-1951

Wage or Salary Recipients	1951	1950	1949	1948	1947	1945	1939
Lowest fifth	3.0	2.3	2.6	2.9	2.9	2.9	3.4
Second fifth	10.6	9.7	10.1	10.2	10.3	10.1	8.4
Middle fifth	18.9	18.3	18.7	18.6	17.8	17.4	15.0
Fourth fifth	25.9	25.7	26.2	25.5	24.7	25.7	23.9
Highest fifth	41.6	44.0	42.4	42.8	44.3	43.9	49.3
TOTAL	100.0	100.0	100.0	100.0	100.0	100.0	100.0

Source: Herman P. Miller, *Income of the American People* (New York: John Wiley & Sons, 1955), Table 54, p. 104.

[21] One of the few published projections of changes in per capita income distribution appeared in *Nation's Business*, July 1956, pp. 44-45. This projection, for the period 1956-1965, is based upon an average annual rate of about 1.8 per cent and varies from less than 1.5 per cent at the upper end of the income scale to more than 4.0 per cent at the lower end.

In projecting the future income distribution for the PSMA, two sets of calculations were made, each based on a different assumption regarding the apportionment of the anticipated increases in income. In the first calculation, it was assumed that all families would experience the average rate of change, and in

Table XIX

EFFECT OF INCREASE IN REAL INCOME ON FAMILY
INCOME DISTRIBUTION OF HOUSEHOLDS
PHILADELPHIA STANDARD METROPOLITAN
AREA, 1957-1970
(Per cent)

| | | Projected Income Distribution 1970 | |
| | | Assumption I | Assumption II |
Income Class	Actual Distribution 1957	20 Per cent Increase Same for All Income Classes	20 Per cent Increase Higher for Lower Income Classes
Under $2,000	11.9	9.9	9.0
$2,000-$3,999	20.1	14.7	15.0
$4,000-$4,999	16.9	9.6	8.0
$5,000-$5,999	15.4	14.7	16.9
$6,000-$6,999	9.7	13.4	16.7
$7,000-$7,999	7.9	9.2	8.1
$8,000-$9,999	8.2	11.8	12.7
$10,000 and over	9.9	16.7	13.6
Total	100.0	100.0	100.0

Percentage Change of Income Class, 1957-1970

Under $5,000	− 30.1	− 38.7
$5,000-$9,999	+19.2	+32.0
$10,000 and up	+68.8	+37.5

the second that the lower income groups would receive a larger share of the increment. The results of these calculations are presented at the bottom of Table XIX. In the income group of $5,000 to $9,999, the estimated range of real income increase from 1957 to 1970 is 19 to 32 per cent; in the $10,000 and over class, the increase ranges from 38 to 69 per cent.

Effect of Income Increase on Market Potential: Estimates of

Table XX

IMPACT OF PROJECTED INCREASES IN REAL INCOME ON DEMAND FOR CENTER CITY HIGH RENT APARTMENTS, 1957-1970

(Per cent)

Income Class	Distribution of Center City Apartment Residents 1957	Assumption I Equal Income Increase All Income Classes		Assumption II Higher Income Increases For Lower Income Classes	
		Projected Household Increase 1957-1970	Weighted Projected Household Increase 1957-1970	Projected Household Increase 1957-1970	Weighted Projected Household Increase 1957-1970
Under $5,000	4.7	−30.1	−1.4	−38.7	−1.8
5,000-9,999	44.9	+19.2	+8.6	+32.0	14.4
10,000 and up	50.4	+68.8	+34.7	+37.5	18.9
TOTAL	100.0	...	+41.9	...	31.5

the overall increase in the high rent market potential from 1957 to 1970 due to shifts in income alone are derived by applying the above projections for the metropolitan area to the current income distribution of center city residents. These calculations indicate a rise in demand of 32 to 42 per cent, depending upon the distribution of the real income increment. (Table XX) The effect of the income increase is to raise the expected range of demand from the 3,200 to 3,400 unit level presented in the previous section to 4,200 to 4,800 units. These estimates assume that: (1) the families who move to higher income levels will not differ significantly with respect to

Table XXI

MEDIAN RATIO OF GROSS RENT TO INCOME BY
INCOME CLASS, FAMILIES AND PRIMARY INDIVIDUALS
LIVING IN HOUSEHOLDS, PHILADELPHIA STANDARD
METROPOLITAN AREA, 1950 AND 1956*
(1950 dollars)

Income Class	1950	1956	1956
Under $2,000	Over 30.0	Over 30.0	Over 30.0
$ 2,000- 3,999	19.0	20.3	22.0
4,000- 4,999	13.9	15.2	16.9
5,000- 5,999	12.7	13.6	15.0
6,000- 6,999	11.4	12.3	13.2
7,000- 9,999	Under 10	10.9	12.1
10,000 and up	**	**	**

Source: 1950 data: Bureau of the Census, *U.S. Census of Housing, 1950*, Bulletin HB-107, Table A-7, p. 9. 1956 data: *1956 National Housing Inventory*, "Philadelphia Supplement," unpublished data.
* Excludes households that occupy dwelling units rent free.
** Not available.

family type, age of head, and employment location from the families presently earning more than $5,000; (2) the same proportion of the various income groups will tend to occupy high rent apartments as today;[22] and (3) there will be no shift

[22] Available evidence suggests that until recently there does not appear to have been any substantial long-run change in the ratio of rent to income despite the fact that construction costs have risen faster than family earnings. Since 1950, however, it appears that the previous trend may have been reversed (Tables XXI and XXII) and that families are now spending more of their income for housing. The procedure employed here, therefore, of projecting constant rent-income ratios to 1970 would seem to be in the direction of conservatism. If construction costs continue to rise more rapidly than real incomes,

in the preference of renters for various residential areas. These assumptions are relaxed later in the chapter.

It thus appears that a substantial proportion of the increase in demand for a high rent central city apartment unit will stem from increments to the real income of Philadelphia's families.

Table XXII

GROSS RENT AS A PER CENT OF INCOME OF FAMILIES AND PRIMARY INDIVIDUALS, PHILADELPHIA STANDARD METROPOLITAN AREA, 1950 AND 1956*

	Per cent of Households	
Rent as a Per cent of Income	1950	1956
Less than 10	9.5	8.3
10-14	21.3	19.5
15-19	22.0	21.4
20-29	24.0	30.8
30 and over	23.2	20.0
TOTAL	100.0	100.0

Source: 1950 data: Bureau of the Census, *U.S. Census of Housing, 1950*, Bulletin HB-107, Table A-3,5 1956 data: *1956 National Housing Inventory*, "Philadelphia Supplement," unpublished data.
* Excludes rent free and incomes over $10,000.

In a very real sense, therefore, the restoration of residential areas in center city on a significant scale is contingent upon the gains in productivity which will materialize in the coming years.

EXPECTED CHANGES IN THE EXISTING STOCK

Replacement demand in a given rent-value stratum of the market is equal to the volume of units that descends into the

however, a portion of the demand projected above may be priced out of the market for new rental units. See Louis Winnick, "Housing: Has There Been a Downward Shift in Consumers' Preferences?" *Quarterly Journal of Economics,* February 1955.

lower rent levels as a result of deterioration and obsolescence plus losses resulting from conversions to smaller or larger apartments, demolitions, and withdrawals of units from residential use. In the highest rent bracket, reduction in the supply due to these changes obviously cannot be compensated by filtration from a higher rental class, and new construction constitutes the only significant means of offsetting these losses.[23]

The importance of obsolescence as a factor in aggregate housing demand is demonstrated by the recent experience in the market for new residential construction. The number of new units built in the Philadelphia area between 1950 and 1957 was almost double the increase in the number of families in the income brackets that could afford these units. The excess units were absorbed by families who left older dwellings that they no longer considered appropriate in size, location, or quality. The older units, in turn, dropped relatively in value and became available to lower income groups.

The rate of decline in the relative value and quality of the standing stock as new construction comes on the market varies greatly with the location, architecture, and quality of construction of both the new and the existing units. Residential units that are well located, planned, and executed may maintain or even improve their relative position on the housing value scale over the years, whereas other units that may have rented for the same amount initially but which were less intelligently conceived may begin descending in value almost immediately upon completion. The volume and price of ensuing construction is at least of equal importance in determining the rate of filtration of the existing stock.[24] A given unit will improve its relative position if new units are introduced at lower rent or value levels; its position will decline if new construction is at higher

[23] Other minor sources of change in the supply of dwellings in this rent class include rehabilitation and the shifting of single family units between the ownership and rental markets.

[24] Ernest M. Fisher and Louis Winnick, "A Reformulation of the Filtering Concept," *Journal of Social Issues*, VII, Nos. 1 and 2 (1951).

levels. For these reasons, a study such as this which examines a particular sector of the market cannot utilize general data on filtering, but must focus specifically on the deterioration likely to be experienced by the units under study.

Changes in the quality of existing luxury apartments in downtown Philadelphia have not conformed with the general patterns of the housing inventory as a whole in recent years. Because these apartments occupy prime sites and have been in great demand, it has been economical to maintain most of them at a level competitive with new construction. If this maintenance policy is continued, these units could remain among the more desirable places to live for an indefinite period into the future. In this event, as few as 200 to 300 units would decline in value to a point where they would cease to appeal to upper income families.

On the other hand, the present apartment expansion along the Parkway and the proposed construction in Society Hill could bring about a significant change in tastes and a concomitant shift of high income renters away from the Rittenhouse Square area. Such shifts in locational preferences have occurred in the past, not only in Philadelphia but in every major American city. If either the development along the Parkway or the redevelopment program in Society Hill were to have this impact on preferences, as many as 2,000 dwelling units could filter to a point where they were no longer in competition with new construction. This would not necessarily mean huge vacancies and rent declines in the existing structures, for a small rent adjustment relative to new construction would expand the market sufficiently to maintain a high rate of occupancy.

Which, if either, of the above two possibilities seems the more likely—relatively little or mass filtering? The answer in this case appears to lie somewhere between these extremes. Almost all the high grade apartment units are concentrated in fewer than twenty structures. Information gathered from inspection of the structures and from interviews with residents, owners, and managers suggests that some of the buildings are destined to filter regardless of what happens to locational preferences, whereas others show a strong likelihood of retaining a position competitive with new construction, even if there is a general movement of high income families to other areas. First, there is a group of about 1,750 luxury units with rents considerably in excess of the level contemplated for new construction. Even if the Rittenhouse Square area were to lose its position as center of the downtown market, these units would not drop below the luxury level for some time to come.

At the other end of the scale, another group of approximately 950 units appears to be on the verge of filtering out of the new construction class regardless of what happens to the rest of the area. The units presently are just barely at new construction rent levels. Among the families who were interviewed in this study there were many who had moved from these units because the managements have pursued maintenance policies which do not effectively combat deterioration. The structures are no longer so neat, clean, and modern in appearance as they were previously. Rather than modernize, managers of these structures have gradually converted some of their units to furnished apartments for transient clientele.

In addition to the 950 units that seem destined to move to lower relative rent status, and 1,750 that appear virtually certain to remain in the highest rent group, there are approximately 300 units whose fate is not presently indicated either by current management policies or taste trends. Thus, depending upon the ultimate disposition of these units, the range of replacement demand should be from 950 to 1,250 units.

Adding this estimate of replacement to the previous calculations of demand, stemming from an increase in households, employment, and income, yields a still higher projection of the market for high rent apartments in center city. This indicates that by 1970 there will be demand for between 5,150 and 6,050 units, a range equivalent to a new construction requirement of 2,150 to 3,050 high rent apartments.

THE BACKLOG OF DEMAND

Demand for new rental housing due to changes in basic long-term factors normally increases or decreases at a small and steady, if not constant, rate. Large rental projects, on the other hand, augment the market supply in discrete and irregularly spaced amounts. Even in cities such as New York and Washington where rental housing constitutes the majority of the supply, the volume of new rental construction is usually much greater than the accretions in demand during the marketing period itself. Because the construction of a large apartment house, unlike the development of a tract of homes, cannot be phased out to absorb the additions to demand as they occur, developers have a tendency to wait until an accumulation of demand is clearly evident. Changes in the availability of financing and problems of site acquisition also contribute to the wide variations in the flow of rental construction.

This sporadic pattern prevailed in central Philadelphia during the past two decades. Between 1939 and 1950 no new apartments were constructed. In the latter year, 940 units were built and filled without difficulty. There then followed a period of seven years during which new construction consisted of only 99 luxury, 299 co-operative, and 119 economy units, all of which appealed to narrow sectors of the market. It was not until 1957, when 1,300 additional units were placed under permit, that projects with a broad market were initiated.

It would appear from this schedule of development that demand for rental housing in central Philadelphia was not fully satisfied by the 940 units constructed in the early 1950's; most certainly additional demand has been accumulating since then. Evidence of a backlog is not difficult to find. A special vacancy survey of all high rent downtown apartments, undertaken as part of this study in January of 1958, found that most of the structures had a waiting list of applicants and no vacancies. The overall vacancy rate was less than 1 per cent.

It is estimated that latent demand generated by increases in households, employment, and income between 1953 and 1957 was sufficient to have absorbed 400 to 600 downtown apartments had they been provided during that period. On the basis of the reported rate of attrition in waiting lists and the length of time that elapsed since the completion of the last major rental developments, it is estimated that approximately one-half of the demand has now been permanently diverted to other areas. The backlog of families still seeking a downtown address is thus at most 200 to 300. This amount, added to the previous demand estimate, raises the total market potential for 1970 from a range of 5,160 to 6,050 to a range of 5,360 to 6,350.

THE PREFERENCE FOR CENTER CITY LIVING

The sources of demand for high rent center city apartments considered up to this point stem from major economic and social trends in the metropolitan region. While the redevelopment effort in center city is not likely to alter the broad metropolitan patterns to a significant extent, it can be of considerable importance in generating interest and, therefore, in expanding demand for housing in the downtown area. In fact, to a limited degree this has already occurred. During the past few years the market has been augmented by a shift in housing preferences among families who, prior to the recent improvements in the central core, would have selected homes in other sections of the city or in the suburbs. In the mass, the net force of this movement has been slight. There can be no doubt, however, that the redevelopment of Washington Square East will draw families to center city who would not otherwise have seriously considered downtown Philadelphia as a place of residence. The area will contain virtually the only high rent apartments east of

Broad Street, and thus will attract families who have previously avoided center city because the upper income residential structures along Rittenhouse Square and the Parkway were not convenient to their respective places of work. The area will also have an environment different from both of the other two sections and will, therefore, tap a new sector of the market on this account also.

All of these factors are buttressed by the fact that downtown Philadelphia as a whole is increasing in attractiveness as a place to live. Compared with a decade ago, it is cleaner, has more green space, and contains a greater number of desirable apartments and single family units. The scope and scale of existing private and public development plans will serve to enhance the area even further. The areas to the north and west of Society Hill are both scheduled for renewal and further development is due between City Hall and the Schuylkill River. The extent to which these improvements will augment the market, however, will depend upon a number of factors which are discussed and assessed in the following sections.

The Question of Changing Preferences: We have previously observed that the number of households occupying high rent apartments in the area is increasing and many of the families moving into these apartments come from other sections of the city. Almost 60 per cent of center city apartment dwellers previously resided in other parts of Philadelphia or in the suburbs.[25] (Table XXIII) Moreover, the inventory of high rent apartments has approximately doubled in the last seven years without producing any vacancies. These data on inmigration

---

[25] By comparison, 28 per cent of the occupants of controlled high rent apartments in Manhattan in November 1956 previously resided outside of Manhattan (*High Rent Housing and Rent Control in New York City, op. cit.*, pp. 89-90). Similar results were reported a year later when a survey of 275 residents of Coliseum Park, a newly constructed apartment building in New York, one block from Columbus Circle, showed that 6 per cent came from suburban counties in New York State, 4 per cent from other states, and 23 per cent from New York City residences outside of Manhattan (*New York Times*, November 21, 1957).

Table XXIII

PREVIOUS PLACE OF RESIDENCE OF HOUSEHOLDS
LIVING IN CENTER CITY HIGH RENT APARTMENTS
DECEMBER 1957

Previous Location	Per cent of Total Households
Center City	33.9
Other Philadelphia	41.1
Outlying Counties, PSMA	17.7
Outside PSMA	7.3
TOTAL	100.0

and population growth in themselves, however, cannot be considered the measure of a rising trend back from the suburbs.

Evidence of changing preferences is present only if the net addition to the number of upper income downtown renters exceeds that which would be expected to occur as a direct consequence of population, income, and employment growth. The preference shift may relate to a change in location, tenure, the proportion of income to be spent for housing, or to all three variables. It need not necessarily involve an actual uprooting of suburban families who otherwise would have stayed where they are. Instead the shift may take place as a result of reduced outmigration from center city, or the influx of a larger percentage of inmigrants to the metropolitan area, or the attraction of a greater share of the families who move from one residence to another within the metropolitan area.

There are a number of factors which affect the volume of demand generated by a shift in consumer preferences. Foremost, perhaps, is the size of the potential market within which the shift must take place. Camel cigarettes have a larger market potential, quantitatively, than Cadillacs, and Levittown can draw from a larger income group than can Washington Square East. Also of considerable importance is the firmness with which existing preferences are held; that is, the strength of the attachment to a particular manufactured product or to a social value such as home ownership or to a given neighborhood in the city. This is a function, in part, of the extent to which consumers feel that the product they now use is distinguished from and superior to any others of comparable price. Still another factor, one which is responsible for much of the shift in preferences observed today, is merchandising effort. In the marketing of apartments in Society Hill, advertising and salesmanship may be especially vital because the commodity being sold will not yet be in existence. Families must be persuaded to move to the area in anticipation of an environment that will fully materialize only at a much later date. It must be clearly recognized that the amenities that will assure the permanent long run success of the project will not be present in the early years. Finally, a fourth factor which should be noted is the cost which a shift in preferences may involve. For example, many families who could afford an air conditioning unit, and who would prefer it to the fan they now have, do not purchase the extra comfort for they feel it is not worth the additional cost. In the housing market, this situation seems most pronounced and is exacerbated by the expense of moving to a new residence. Thus, latent preferences for Society Hill may build up at a considerably faster pace than families move to the area.

The extent to which the skilled merchandising of a massive residential improvement can influence the thinking and actions of families who enter the residential market simply cannot be forecast with any certainty. Nor is it possible to estimate with precision how the other variables described above will interact to produce a preference shift of a given magnitude. There are, however, reasonable limits which may be assigned on the basis of recent experience and on the size of the potential market. The remainder of this chapter, therefore, is directed to an examination of these two factors in an attempt to arrive at an estimate of the general level of preference shift that is consistent with known facts.

Recent Preference Shifts: It has become commonplace to point to the trend in population movement from the city to the outlying areas, but it is well to be reminded of the strength of the movement. In 1955 and 1956, more than 23,000 families moved from Philadelphia to the suburban counties while only 3,300 moved from the suburbs to the city. Of the families who moved to the metropolitan area from elsewhere, 22,600 moved to the suburbs and only 5,700 to the city. (Table XXIV) Although the implications of the aggregate data for the city as a whole are unmistakable, there are two sections which may be

Table XXIV

PRESENT AND PREVIOUS PLACE OF RESIDENCE OF
HOUSEHOLDS THAT MOVED IN 1955 AND 1956,
BY RACE, PHILADELPHIA STANDARD
METROPOLITAN AREA

	PRESENT PLACE OF RESIDENCE					
	Philadelphia City			Suburbs		
	Race			Race		
Previous Place of Residence	White	Non-White	Total	White	Non-White	Total
Philadelphia	55,757	34,178	89,935	22,465	581	23,046
Suburbs	2,576	757	3,333	68,561	5,893	74,454
Outside PSMA	5,461	214	5,675	22,136	484	22,620
NA	874	19	893	1,701	0	1,701
TOTAL	64,668	35,168	99,836	114,863	6,958	121,821

Source: U.S. Bureau of the Census, *1956 National Housing Inventory*, Philadelphia Supplement, unpublished data.

running counter to the trend. One is the far northeastern section of the city which can be considered suburban in character and thus part of the general pattern of population dispersion, and the other is the central city area itself.

The direction and rate of shift to the central core over the past few years were calculated in the following manner: First, using the same methods that were employed to project demand to 1970, an estimate was made of the increase in demand for high rent apartments in center city from 1943, the year housing came into short supply, to 1957. This estimate was then compared with the actual number of units absorbed during the fourteen-year interval plus the backlog of demand still in existence at the end of the period. The difference represented the number of units of demand that could be attributed to changing preferences. This calculation yielded an estimate of 300 to 400 units. Thus, between 1943 and 1957, roughly 20 to 25 per cent of the demand for new rental units in downtown Philadelphia was attributable to a shift in the pattern of preferences of the community. In absolute numbers, the volume is small indeed, even if the entire shift in attitudes is assumed to have occurred during a shorter period.

Because of the paucity of data for the period 1943 to 1950, the estimate cited above is, at best, quite crude. As an aggregate figure it also fails to reveal any information regarding the trend over time. It is not known, for example, whether the change in attitudes toward center city began with the construction of 2601 Parkway twenty years ago, or with the erection of the Savoy, Claridge, and Parkway House around 1951. And since there has been little construction since 1951, we may not have an accurate view of what has happened to preferences since that time. Even more important, we do not know to what extent the figure reflects a shortage of housing, either downtown or elsewhere, that made it impossible for the true preferences of many families to have an opportunity for expression in the market place. Finally, we do not know whether the preference shift occurred among a group in the population that now consists primarily of downtown dwellers or whether it took place among family types that are found predominantly outside of center city. If the latter proves to be the case it could herald a major new trend of significant proportions. Withal, we can be sure of only one thing: If there has been a change in preferences, it has indeed been modest, for the pressure on supply which would have resulted from a significant shift has not been observed to any measurable degree.[26]

Reservoir of Demand: The number of families that may be drawn into the center city in response to the improvements and innovations described above is related to the size of the reservoir of families whose preferences are most susceptible to change if center city residential areas are properly planned and merchandised.

There appears to be little hope of attracting families with school age children to center city apartment houses. The view that "the high rise structure is no place to rear children" was voiced even by the families with youngsters living in such buildings, and these sentiments were also expressed by several apartment managers. Where families with growing children can afford it, they move into the home ownership market. Not only is it a matter of atmosphere and environment; housing space can be acquired in these areas at a considerably lower outlay per room than in a downtown apartment. A family with two or three children seeking a three bedroom downtown apartment will be confronted with a rental of $250 or more a month, while in a new development of single family homes the same space can be obtained at half the cost. It comes as no surprise, therefore, to learn that there were children in less than 6 per cent of the high priced center city apartment units.

If households with children are entirely eliminated from the

[26] This was written before data were available on the market impact of Ambassador Towne House and Park Towne Place. Vacancy data collected after these apartments appeared on the market tend to confirm the finding that the preference shift has indeed been quite moderate.

downtown apartment market, there are still 68,000 families in the Philadelphia Standard Metropolitan Area who possess income, age, household composition, and employment characteristics that mark them as highly potential customers.[27] Yet, less than 4 per cent of these families presently live in high rent downtown units. Where are the rest?

Approximately 55,000 are home owners. Slightly more than 13,000 are renters, of whom 11,000 reside in lower quality apartments, and 2,000 live in competitively priced rental structures located outside the central city.

If only a modest percentage of the home owners were persuaded to change their preferences, the demand for center city units would double. To achieve even a small proportion may not be simple, however. Home ownership and residence in a single family home are among the strongest and most widely held of American values and aspirations. Even elderly couples without children, widows, and widowers, who do not need a six or seven-room house, tend to cling to this type of home, nevertheless.[28] There are strong personal attachments to the structure itself and to all of the neighborhood associations. In addition, these families enjoy a garden of their own and such advantages as extra space for visits by the children and grandchildren. If they moved into an apartment, many of these advantages would have to be sacrificed and, at the same time, there is a strong possibility that housing costs would be increased.

This is not to suggest that the single family home is an in-

[27] For further details, the reader may wish to re-examine Tables III through VIII.

[28] Mobility data for the Philadelphia Standard Metropolitan Area gathered in connection with the *National Housing Inventory* show that the middle-aged and elderly groups in the population tend to move considerably less frequently than do younger persons. On the average, almost 50 per cent of all households with heads under 35 moved during the three-year period, 1954-1956, as compared with only 30 per cent of those with heads 35 to 44, 16 per cent of those with heads 45-64, and less than 10 per cent of those with heads 65 and over.

vincible citadel. In large sections of Philadelphia and in parts of the suburbs as well, the homes are between forty and sixty years old and well on the way to deterioration and obsolescence. In these neighborhoods the environment ranges from one of faded gentility to incipient slum, and improvement is not in sight. Many of the occupants of these aging areas no longer find either their homes or their neighborhood suitable, and they have and will continue to cast about for a new abode. Since they are surrounded by built-up sections that may be as old and even less desirable than the one in which they now live, they have the option of moving out to newer areas, or moving into the center. The younger families with children will tend to the former choice. Some of the older groups, though, may rebel against the more onerous and expensive journey to work that would be associated with a residence farther out. Equally, many may object to paying increasing taxes for schools and other facilities that their families do not use. They could be drawn downtown, provided the accommodations and the area are suitable and attractive.[29]

At present, however, when home owners decide to move to rental accommodations, a majority prefer the outlying to the downtown apartment houses. Interviews revealed that of more than 5,000 former owners living in high rent accommodations throughout Philadelphia only 1,300 are in center city as compared with roughly 3,900 in the outlying apartment houses. Although a desire to remain in a familiar environment played an important role in the choice of new residence, as we shall shortly see, atmosphere of the surroundings may also have been a factor. Even among the occupants of downtown apartments, the influence of environmental differences were apparent; 54 per cent of the renters of the apartments on the Parkway as

[29] This type of shift is taking place in New York City where it has been a prominent factor in the movement of high income families from the west side to the east side of Manhattan. The movement in Manhattan is also due in part to the desire of many families for a prestige address.

against 29 per cent in the Rittenhouse Square area were former home owners.[30] The relatively greater success of the former units in attracting home owners appears to have been due in part to the existence of open, planted surroundings.

In the rental market, the group that constitutes the most likely source of demand for the high rent center city apartments consists of 11,000 families who enjoy substantial incomes, but who occupy apartments of modest or inferior quality. Some of these families devote a small proportion of their income to rent because of the burden of financial obligations, but for most of the group the available housing cannot compete successfully against other commodities (or savings) as an outlet for their incomes. For some, it is a matter of the strong positive attractiveness of a trip abroad, or superior entertainment, or fine clothes, while for others it is the fact that the available high rent housing does not offer an improvement in quality, location, or status commensurate with the required increase in rent.

Thus, this group of more than 11,000 renter families contains many who may be waiting for better apartments to come on the market. There is little doubt that this group can be influenced by an intelligently conceived advertising campaign which will alter their expenditure patterns in favor of housing, but it can be seen that a substantial proportion will have to be reached to have an important effect on total demand.

In contrast to the previous group, very little shift in preferences can be expected to issue from the 2,000 renters mentioned above who occupy apartments in outlying areas that are comparable in quality with the more expensive center city units. Interviews with a sample of the residents of these apartments revealed their firm rejection of downtown living as they visualized it at the time of the interview. Ninety-five per cent of the respondents answered "no" when asked if they would have rented an identical apartment in downtown Philadelphia,

---

[30] In the downtown area as a whole, 44 per cent of the occupants of high rent apartments were former home owners.

were one available at the time they moved to their present quarters. Moreover, all but a few stated that they felt the same way at the time of the interview. Further evidence of their tie to the area is seen in the fact that slightly more than one-half of the residents of outlying apartments had previously lived within a short distance of their present residence. Thus, this group does not appear to constitute a likely source for the expansion of the central city market in the near future.

Cutting across the tenure classification, there is another group of families whose preferences might be changed. It will be remembered that about 20 per cent of the households interviewed in center city had at least one, but not all of the four characteristics—income, age, household composition, and employment—of the major demand group. In fact, in the population at large there are many families whose characteristics resemble very closely those of center city apartment residents. It would seem, in particular, that some of the household heads who have all the characteristics of downtown residents, except that they are employed near but not in center city, could be persuaded that downtown Philadelphia is pleasant as well as a convenient place in which to live.[31] Within two miles from center city there are approximately 15,000 such employed individuals who do not live in the central area. For many of these persons downtown Philadelphia is more convenient to their job locations than are their present homes. Members of this group could considerably shorten their work journeys, and some could perhaps walk to work as do many of the present downtown residents. Moreover, regardless of whether they used public or private transportation, they would be travelling counter to the peak traffic movements.

Implications for the Future: The major observation to emerge from this analysis is that, in recent years, the market

---

[31] Included in this group, for example, would be many of the faculty and administrative personnel of the University of Pennsylvania, Drexel Institute, and Temple University.

for new rental construction in central Philadelphia has been slightly larger than would have been predicted on the basis of economic factors alone. Among the elements that account for this difference is a shift in preference in favor of center city living, and it would appear that downtown Philadelphia can continue to draw upon this source of demand for some time in the future. This additional demand will, however, be of modest dimension because the reservoir of families who might be persuaded to live downtown is but a small proportion of the metropolitan area population, and also because housing tenure and location preferences of families are rather firmly held. For the period 1957 to 1970 we expect demand from shifting preferences to reach 1,000 to 1,500 units, or approximately 20 to 30 per cent of the total projected demand growth. This estimate is based upon fragmentary data for past years coupled with the visualization of an environment not yet created and upon the evaluation of the extent to which families will readjust their attitudes toward housing, as the face and form of the urban structure undergo gradual transformation.

DOWNTOWN APARTMENT DEMAND 1957-1970—A SUMMARY

The burden of this chapter has been devoted to the derivation of an estimate of the demand for new rental construction in central Philadelphia for the thirteen-year period, January 1957 to January 1970. The various factors influencing demand were described in detail and quantified. This final section presents a recapitulation of the major factors contributing to an expansion of the market for new rental units and a brief evaluation of the findings insofar as the redevelopment program for Society Hill is concerned. (Table XXV) A more extensive analysis of the market implications for Society Hill is presented in Chapter VI.

Household Growth: Aggregate demand as of January 1957 was estimated to be 3,000 units. Based upon demographic

Table XXV

SOURCES OF INCREMENTAL DEMAND FOR HIGH RENT
APARTMENTS IN CENTER CITY PHILADELPHIA,
1957 TO 1970

	Number of Households (Range of Estimate)	
Source of Demand	Low	High
Population Growth and Employment Redistribution	200	400
Income Change	1,000	1,400
Obsolescence of Existing Center City Supply	950	1,250
Backlog of Demand	200	300
Preference Changes	1,000	1,500
Vacancy Allowance	300	400
TOTAL	3,650	5,250

projections it was found that the type of household characteristic of present central city apartment occupants would increase by approximately 20 per cent, a growth equivalent to a demand of 600 units.

Employment Distribution: The major source of demand comes from individuals either employed in the central city or not in the labor force. The estimate above assumes that the distribution of employment will not change between 1957 and 1970. It is expected, however, that employment in central city will not rise as rapidly as in other sections of the metropolitan area. The maximum projected increase is 10 per cent while the rise for the entire Philadelphia area is estimated at 14 per cent. This slower rate of employment growth in the CBD will be offset to some extent by a more than proportionate increase in the retired sector of the population, and by an increase in the proportion of upper income white collar jobs. But the net effect is a reduction of the previous estimate of demand by 200 to 400 units.

Income Change: The estimate above was revised upward to account for changes in the distribution of family income in the metropolitan area and for an estimated growth in real income of approximately 1.5 per cent per year. These two factors in combination are expected to increase demand by 32 to 42 per cent, or approximately 1,000 to 1,400 units.

Obsolescence of Supply: The number of downtown units that will filter out of the high rent brackets between 1957 and 1970 was estimated to be in the range of 950 to 1,250 units, depending upon shifts in consumer preferences and upon maintenance policies of apartment owners.

Backlog of Demand: The volume of apartment construction in downtown Philadelphia in recent years has been less than the increase in the number of families who would desire to locate in the area. A calculation revealed the backlog of demand to be in the vicinity of 200 to 300 units.

Preference Changes: There has been a small but gradual increase in the preference patterns of Philadelphia households in favor of center city living. Since the war, this has averaged approximately 50 units per year, and with improvements to come in downtown Philadelphia, it is expected that demand for 1,000 to 1,500 additional dwelling units will accrue from this source.

Vacancy Allowance: Allowance must be made in the calculation of demand for a vacancy rate that will permit the consumer a sufficient choice of units and yet not be so large as to endanger the stability of the market. A vacancy rate of 4.5 to 5.0 per cent of the entire stock is considered satisfactory in this sector of housing supply. To maintain such a rate, 300 to 400 additional units will be required.

Implications: The cumulative effect of the demand factors presented above indicates a market increase between 1957 and 1970 of 3,650 to 5,250 high rent center city apartment units.

This is equivalent to an average rate of expansion of 280 to 400 units annually, and equals roughly 8 to 12 per cent of total rental construction estimated for the metropolitan area for this period.[32] The absorption of units will not, however, follow an even pattern. Because of the backlog of demand which existed as of January 1957, and which continued to build up until April 1958 when the Ambassador Towne House became available for occupancy, the marketing rate for new construction in the current year (1958) is calculated to be in the range of 800 to 1,200 units. The pace of demand will then drop sharply to an average of approximately 200 to 300 units annually until the apartments in Society Hill are introduced into the market. If these units have the consumer appeal that is assumed in our calculations, their contribution to the center city market will raise the annual rate of absorption to approximately 300 to 400 units yearly.

[32] See *Demand for Housing in the Eastwick Redevelopment Area* (Institute for Urban Studies, University of Pennsylvania, 1959).

IV

The Market for Single Family Homes

The apartment house construction planned for Society Hill will be accompanied by the development of a community of approximately 430 new and rehabilitated single family homes. These units, ranging in price from $16,000 to $75,000, will contribute to the expansion of a pattern of downtown residential development that has emerged in Philadelphia and in other American cities in recent years.[1]

There are in central Philadelphia today approximately 600[2] homes of high quality that provide a pleasant living environment and convenient location for middle and upper income families. About 450 are located south of Market Street between Broad Street and the Schuylkill River. A lesser number, approximately 100, are in an area directly east of Broad extending as far as Ninth Street. The remainder are found in small scattered clusters, some in Society Hill itself and others north of Market Street.

A few of the homes are of post-World War II construction and several date from the 1920's. The vast majority, however, are of pre-twentieth century vintage. Many of the older units, until quite recently, were slum dwellings occupied by families in the lowest income brackets. Yet families and private redevelopers with vision and fortitude, sensing a future in downtown Philadelphia, moved into these areas a house or two at a time and rehabilitated the structures for personal use, rent, or resale.

[1] See William H. Whyte, Jr., "Are Cities Un-American?" *Fortune*, September, 1957.

[2] This estimate is based on a field inspection of the entire central area, supported by 1950 census block statistics, and calculations of new construction, rehabilitation, conversions, and demolitions occurring since 1950.

90

Gradually, sections of the slums were pushed back and replaced by well-built and, in many instances, exceptionally attractive homes. In the past decade, 400 single family residences have been subjected to major rehabilitation. In addition, the owners of many sound but dowdy buildings have been spurred into general conservation efforts, façade modernization, and higher levels of maintenance.

Considerable variety is found among the rehabilitated units. There are bandboxes that possess much charm but little space, federal houses that are substantial but unostentatious, and large and impressive town houses of obvious value. Some stand flush with the building line, while others face on internal courts that afford a considerable degree of privacy. Virtually all are located on minor streets on which there is no through traffic. In today's market these units range in value from $12,000 to over $50,000. (Table XXVI)

One-tenth of the single family units are renter occupied. The contract rent (which does not include heat, water, or utilities) is $110 or less in over 90 per cent of these cases. This places the value of the bulk of the rented units under $15,000 where they constitute the large majority of the inventory. Virtually all of the renter occupied units, therefore, fall below the value levels contemplated in Society Hill.

The redevelopment plan which provides for a two-thirds increase in the total present supply of 600 units will thus increase the number of higher quality owner-occupied units (over $15,000) by three-fourths. In this context, the 400 new units, trivial in Philadelphia's total housing picture, become a major factor indeed in the downtown market. Since rehabilitation will continue in other parts of center city, it is conceivable that the number of high priced single family units in the downtown area will more than double in the next decade.

The method used to estimate the demand for single family units parallels the analysis and projection of the demand for high rise apartments outlined in the previous chapter. The

Table XXVI

INVENTORY OF MEDIUM AND HIGH VALUE SINGLE
FAMILY HOMES IN CENTER CITY PHILADELPHIA, 1957

	Number	Per cent
A. Composition		
New Construction	50	8
Major Rehabilitation	400	67
Minor or No Rehabilitation	150	25
TOTAL	600	100
B. Value		
$12,000-14,999	130	22
15,000-19,999	145	24
20,000-24,999	185	31
25,000 and Over	140	23
TOTAL	600	100
C. Tenure		
Owned	540	90
Rented	60	10
TOTAL	600	100
D. Location		
West of Broad and South of Market	450	75
East of Broad and South of Market	100	17
North of Market	50	8
TOTAL	600	100

Source: Field surveys by ACTION and by the Institute for Urban Studies.

field survey of center city home owners and data derived from the Philadelphia supplement to the *National Housing Inventory* made it possible to identify the characteristics of this segment of the market and determine its current numbers in the total metropolitan area. Projections of the growth of this group constituted the first approximation of demand. Adjustments were then made for preference shifts and for competition from other residential renewal activity in center city. Finally, the estimates were translated into demand schedules showing the probable annual marketing rate of variously priced homes in a well-conceived development in the Society Hill area.

HOUSEHOLD CHARACTERISTICS

The single family home owners in center city are remarkably similar to the residents of the neighboring high rise apartment structures. Over 90 per cent of the household heads are over 35 years of age.[3] Ninety per cent work in center city or do not work at all. Eighty-five per cent of the households have no children, and 95 per cent have no children of school age. Eighty per cent of the families have annual incomes in excess of $5,000; and of the families whose homes are valued at $16,000 or more, the contemplated price class for Society Hill, this ratio is 90 per cent. The proportion of families having all four characteristics is in excess of 70 per cent. Thus, the single family home market in center city apparently draws from the same groups as the apartment market. It differs from the apartment sector in that it attracts a slightly higher proportion of families that do not have all four of the key characteristics. But other than this, there is little to differentiate the two groups of demanders. Nevertheless, the two markets appear to be quite distinct. Of a sample of 124 residents of high rise apartments, none was previously an owner of a moderate or high quality

[3] In contrast, over 50 per cent of the renters of single family homes are under 35. In virtually all other respects the renters closely resemble the owner-occupant group.

single family unit in center city; and of 79 owners, only three had moved from a high rise downtown apartment. The absence of contact between the two markets indicates that the sale of single family units will not be impaired by the simultaneous rental of nearby apartment units.

PROJECTION OF HOUSEHOLD GROWTH, EMPLOYMENT, AND INCOME

Because of the close similarity between the two groups of potential demanders, the income, employment, and household growth projections calculated for the apartment market were applied to the home ownership sector. In the previous chapter it was noted that these three factors in combination would increase the downtown market for high rent apartments by 40 to 60 per cent between 1957 and 1970. Applying this projection to the current inventory of 450 single family homes valued at $16,000 or more, yields, as a first approximation, a demand for 630 to 720 one family units in center city thirteen years hence. The incremental demand of 180 to 270 units implies a modest rate of increase of 15 to 20 units a year for the entire central area. This amount will, however, be augmented by the demand factors described below.

CHANGES IN THE EXISTING STOCK

Ordinarily, the sheer passage of time has the effect of causing deterioration and consequent filtration of at least some portion of the housing inventory. Changing tastes, improved products, and concomitant obsolescence typically accelerate the process. In center city, however, extremely few single family units of higher value are in the process of filtering down, and much of the substandard stock is being raised to high quality by large doses of additional investment. Moreover, demolition occurring in connection with presently planned redevelopment will make virtually no inroads in the existing supply of higher priced units. Some conversion to nonresidential and multi-family use will take place, but the number of withdrawals for these purposes has been very small in recent years and is not expected to increase. In general, therefore, little replacement demand is anticipated. In the thirteen-year period, it is not likely to go beyond the range of 25 to 50 units.

CHANGING PREFERENCES[4]

It is evident from the preceding analysis that the single family home market in Society Hill, like that for high rise apartments, cannot depend for its success on general expansionary factors in the local economy. For the contemplated number of homes to be sold within a reasonable period of time, the area must draw a greater share of its market potential to center city than has been captured in the past. In this effort it will be in a much better position than the high rise apartments; with reasonably attractive homes and site planning, there should be no difficulty in disposing of all 430 homes by 1970 or sooner.

This conclusion is not immediately apparent from the record of residential renewal in center city in recent years. Rehabilitation and new construction, although producing improvements over a wide area, have actually occurred at a moderate pace. Net additions to the inventory of single family homes valued at more than $16,000 are estimated to have been no more than 10 to 15 units annually. The rise in the number of upper income families has also been modest.[5] Fully one-half of the occupants of medium and high priced units in center city were already living in their present homes when the improvement

---

[4] This section leans heavily on the discussion of changing preferences presented in Chapter III.

[5] The reader will, of course, recognize that it is possible to have had a rehabilitation program without any increase in the high income population in the area if the resident families alone were responsible for the improvements. The converse is also true.

program gained momentum around 1950. Of the more recent arrivals it is estimated that at least one-quarter simply replaced outmigrant families of equivalent incomes. Thus the expansion of the area, whether expressed in terms of increments to physical supply or as increases in the number of well-to-do families, has been quite slow.

Although the rate of improvement has been modest, it was achieved in the face of several serious obstacles. First, for many years it was difficult to obtain financing from institutional sources for the acquisition and reconstruction of the slum dwellings. Second, business logic indicates that small-scale private rehabilitation must be attached to a core of good homes so that the improved block can become part of a better neighborhood. The majority of homes in the new blocks must, therefore, be brought up to standard before the areas beyond become eligible for investment. The smooth spread of this development has been hindered by a rapid rise in the price of old houses and by difficulties encountered in attempting to acquire homes held by estates or by owners who do not wish to move. Expansion has also been halted by physical barriers, such as major traffic arteries, and by nonresidential uses. Third, until relatively recently, it was difficult to find families willing to pioneer blocks in which rehabilitation had just begun, and where decay and danger were not too far removed.

Center city real estate brokers, including those engaged in renewal activity, agree that additions to supply have not kept pace with demand and that a higher rate of rehabilitation could have easily been supported by the market. Their views are, in part, substantiated by the rise in price for slum units. Less than a decade ago, medium-sized houses that now command $4,500 could have been purchased for $500. Thus, it is not the pace of renewal that is the measure of the basic strength of the center city market, but other indicators of demand: the trend in prices and, above all, the flow of investment and families into the area in the face of generally undesirable but improving conditions.

Even in the absence of preference shifts, a set of new conditions, some of which are specific to Society Hill and others the result of developments in central city, will bring about an increase in migration to the area. The sheer availability of substantial additions to the supply of adequate homes will release some of the unsatisfied demand that has accumulated over the years. In addition, the growth in the number of good areas in central city has increased the attractiveness of the entire district and will serve to draw families who wish a downtown residence, but who have been reluctant to live in a generally run-down area simply to achieve the benefits of a central location.

Within this framework, single family units in Society Hill have several competitive advantages, of which scale is perhaps the most important. The renewal area is close to 130 acres in size, large enough to provide its own atmosphere and environment. It will also be more attractive than most residential neighborhoods in center city. Present home owners have been drawn to other sections of the downtown area despite the existence of a number of negative elements. On the days that garbage and trash are collected, the "new look" disappears behind a fortress of cans and rubbish extending almost without interruption from one corner to the next. By most standards, open space, either common or private, is inadequate. The rehabilitation efforts are not of uniformly high quality, nor are they all in good architectural taste. Traffic, dirt, and noise, although not serious problems, are above the tolerance limits of many families. Without doubt, these problems will not exist in redeveloped Society Hill.

Although the favorable position of center city and, particularly, the Society Hill home ownership market is by now quite clear, it may be well to mention three additional factors of some importance.

First, there is a group of families who desire a home of their own, but also insist upon a new unit. Up to the present, these families have been almost completely excluded from the center city market. Approximately 30 per cent of the Society Hill homes will be newly constructed and will serve to attract this sector of the home ownership market.

Second, lack of high quality housing and spread of residential deterioration in some sections of Philadelphia were cited in the previous chapter as a possible source of demand for new rental units in center city. This observation is even more relevant in the ownership market. Families in the upper income brackets seeking a rental unit have a fairly wide choice of high quality apartments in various parts of the city which contain somewhat more than one-half of all apartment units in the metropolitan area renting for $35 or more per room. In the ownership market, on the other hand, nine out of ten houses worth more than $20,000 are to be found in the outlying counties of the PSMA. The suburbs also account for considerably more than half of the homes in the $15,000 to $20,000 price range. A family leaving one of Philadelphia's older neighborhoods or simply looking for an expensive home is, at present, virtually forced into the suburbs. With the redevelopment of Society Hill another alternative to exodus will have been created.

Third, in the ownership market there is the possibility of attracting families with school children, even though the present proportion of such households in center city is quite small. A house, unlike a high rise apartment, appeals to more than a token segment of this market. The relative lack of families with school age children in center city today is attributable primarily to the large volume of commercial, industrial, and adult entertainment activities that interlard the area. While some parents value such surroundings in preparing a child for an urban life, the vast majority do not, and redevelopment will not change their views. Among the amenable group, however, perhaps the most important deterrent is the fact that the existing public school facilities are crowded and do not go beyond the sixth grade. Without doubt an adequate school plant will augment the demand for single family houses, but it is not likely to have any discernible effect on the market for apartment units. Since apartments in high rise or converted structures will constitute 90 per cent of the dwelling units in Society Hill, the child population of the area will never be very large.[6]

The combined influence of all of these factors on the center city market for single family units is not readily quantifiable. The extent to which the market can be expanded is a function not only of the strength of the factors themselves, but also of the size of the market that will be influenced by them. It was previously observed that the potential market rests in a group that has strong predilections for home ownership. Therefore, it would seem much less difficult to attract some of these families to a downtown house than it would be to persuade them to rent an apartment in the same location. Thus, both the supply and demand sides of the equation appear to be extremely favorable, and it does not seem improbable that perhaps two and one-half to three times as much demand will come from shifting preferences as from growth factors alone. This is an increase of 450 to approximately 800 units,[7] and raises the estimate of incremental demand to a range of 655 to 1,130 units for the thirteen-year period.

This estimate can be placed in perspective by comparing it

[6] In the recent past much of the child population has come from the moderate or low income household. These groups have been leaving the area as their economic status increased or as redevelopment compelled them to seek quarters elsewhere. The remaining population, as well as the incoming groups, consist almost exclusively of adults.

[7] In both absolute and relative terms, this represents a much smaller change of preferences than was predicted for the high rise apartments. It should be remembered, however, that the apartment market offers a selection of accommodations covering a wider range of housing types and expenditures.

with a projection of total metropolitan area construction in the same price range. It has been estimated [8] that, from 1957 to 1970, the PSMA housing stock will be augmented by approximately 210,000 new single family homes of which 30 per cent, or almost 65,000, will be priced at $16,000 or more. Therefore, center city need capture less than 2 per cent of the total market for new expensive homes to equal the maximum demand figure that we have projected for the area. It should be cautioned that of the 65,000 new homes, only about 10 per cent will be acquired by families who have the characteristics that would make them likely candidates for a downtown residence. Thus the estimate of the number of home buyers who can be attracted to center city is actually 12 to 18 per cent of the smaller and more realistic market potential figure. Even within this more restricted context, the projection of demand does not seem to be disproportionately large.

CONCLUSIONS AND RECOMMENDATIONS

The demand for medium and high priced single family homes in center city may be expected to expand at an average rate of approximately 50 to 90 units per year over the next decade. Much of this growth will be directly attributable to the availability of attractive new and rehabilitated homes in Society Hill, and the redevelopment site will be the major beneficiary of migration to the downtown area. Whereas residential renewal in other sections of central Philadelphia will be reduced in pace because of the declining number of structures in which investments can profitably be made, the marketing rate in Society Hill will experience an upward trend as the effects of redevelopment become evident to potential home buyers.

[8] *Demand for Housing in the Eastwick Redevelopment Area* (Institute for Urban Studies, University of Pennsylvania. 1959).

Price Levels of New Construction: The present inventory of single family homes in center city contains a heavy concentration of houses in the highest price bracket. Almost 25 per cent are in the most expensive range, $25,000 and up; 30 per cent are valued from $20,000 to $25,000; and another 25 per cent between $16,000 and $20,000. Only one-fifth are valued at less than $16,000. This distribution departs quite radically from the shape of the total demand curve for housing in the PSMA. For the entire metropolitan area, the proportion of homes in each of the above price classes is 3 per cent, 6 per cent, 8 per cent, and 83 per cent, respectively. If the present price distribution in center city is to be maintained in the future, preference shifts, which will account for more than half of total demand, must be considerably more widespread in the high-priced than in the medium-priced market.

The experience to date has been quite the opposite. The pressure of demand appears to be much greater for the lower priced units than for the more expensive dwellings. Homes priced below $20,000 move quickly (less than 30 days) and without difficulty, while luxury dwellings priced at more than $25,000 require intensive selling efforts and, typically, cannot be sold in less than two and one-half to four months in a generally active market. For this reason it is recommended that, initially, the marketing schedule should provide for no more than five units per year at prices in excess of $25,000. In the $20,000 to $25,000 range, the market should be able to absorb 15 to 25 units annually while in the $16,000 to $20,000 bracket, the demand will vary between 30 and 60 units. Society Hill will account for approximately two-thirds of the total, yielding a demand of 35 to 60 units a year and a marketing period of six to ten years.

V

The Demand for Rehabilitated Apartment Units

The third part of the three-pronged residential renewal program in Society Hill consists of the rehabilitation and conversion of approximately 100 structures to multi-family occupancy. Some of these buildings are already in apartment or mixed use, while others are occupied as single family homes. After rehabilitation, these structures will provide 450 to 500 family accommodations. Two major questions face the Redevelopment Authority with respect to these units: First, what is the demand for this type of accommodation; and second, at what rent levels should these units be introduced into the market? It is to these two problems that this chapter is directed.

Like the renewal program for single family units, the addition to the rental supply through rehabilitation represents a continuation of an activity that has been in progress in center city for approximately three decades. The exact number of structures that have been the recipients of major investment outlays during this period is not known, but it is estimated that the number of dwelling units produced in this fashion in the past decade totals approximately 300.

The primary targets for this type of activity have been the large row houses containing ten or more rooms in three or more stories. Occupied as single family units at one time, their size has made it extremely difficult to find ready buyers in the home ownership market. Although a number have remained in single family use over the years, the bulk have been converted to rooming houses or subdivided into apartments. In some cases extensive structural alterations have been made, while in others the conversion has been largely through use by virtue of a change in type of occupancy. In general, however, regardless of occupancy status, these buildings are structurally sound, though lacking in modern floor plans, appointments, fixtures, and equipment.

Structural conversion of these homes to multi-family use has followed no set pattern. The resultant units have ranged from one-room efficiency apartments to family type units containing two or more bedrooms. Some structures were initially remodeled twenty to thirty years ago and refurbished in the 1950's. In these the improvement costs were modest and have been recouped through higher rents, reduced vacancies, and lower turnover. Other structures were converted and rehabilitated for the first time in the postwar period, the bulk since 1950. A recent, but not necessarily typical, case cited by a downtown builder involved the acquisition of an old twelve-room house for $12,500, and its subdivision into seven apartments at a cost of $20,000.

The rents for rehabilitated units vary between $20 and $35 per room per month (plus utilities) depending upon the size and quality of the apartment. On a dwelling unit basis this is equivalent to a range of $65 per month (plus utilities) for a one-bedroom unit to $150 for a three-bedroom apartment, with the vast majority of accommodations falling in the $75 to $125 bracket. Thus, the rents are substantially below the level of new construction where rents are usually in excess of $40 per room. The effective difference between the two rent levels is even greater than these figures indicate because the older units tend to have larger rooms, and, in addition, the rent frequently includes the use of an enclosed yard.

HOUSEHOLD CHARACTERISTICS

The characteristics of the rehabilitated apartments give some clue as to the types of households living in them. The moderate rent levels would suggest lower incomes and the interviews reveal that such is the case; over 30 per cent of the families earn less than $5,000 per year. The larger floor areas and the yard space would be expected to have some appeal to families with children; and indeed 30 per cent do have youngsters, although very few of the children are of school age. The lack of elevator service to the upper floors or the absence of desk service could be presumed to be a deterrent to older persons, so it is not surprising that approximately one-half of the households consist of unmarried individuals under 35 years of age.[1] It is in this sector of the downtown market, rather than in the high rise apartment or in the single family home, that one finds the young single person attracted by the bustle, excitement, and opportunity of the city. In only one respect do these households conform closely to the downtown prototype described in the previous chapters. Approximately 90 per cent of the household heads either work in center city or are not in the labor force.

Expressed in terms of demand groups, the occupants of the rehabilitated units may be divided as follows: One-half of the households consist of single individuals or two or more un-related persons employed in center city; one-quarter are husband and wife households with no school age children and with the heads of these households either employed in center city or retired; a final one-quarter consist of representatives of virtually all other sectors of the population.

Thus, the rehabilitated apartment units draw to a considerably lesser extent from the household types that are to be found in the single family units or in the more expensive rental construction, and to a much greater degree from other sectors of the population. They find a wide market among the younger unmarried individuals who do not desire to spend very much for housing or who are reluctant to sign a long lease or who are not necessarily interested in having a prestige address. They serve the families with children who are not in a position to

---

[1] Of those 35 and under, however, very few are under 25.

own or rent a home and yet need more space than is available in the expensive high rise apartments. In general, the occupants represent a broad range of income and age groups. Competitively, therefore, the rehabilitated units are more or less indistinguishable from other moderately priced downtown apartments that provide accommodations for the renter household.

THE GROWTH MARKET

It is estimated that the current inventory of medium rent apartments ($20 to $35 per room) in downtown Philadelphia totals approximately 3,300 units.[2] By applying the methods that were used in Chapter III in the derivation of the future market for high rise apartments, it was calculated that the demand for centrally located, moderately priced rental accommodations would increase by 15 to 35 per cent, or 500 to 1,150 units, by 1970.

Approximately one-third of the estimated increment will stem from a moderate rise in the number of household heads who work in center city or are retired. The more important source of demand growth will result from augmented real incomes. The increase in income, however, will not affect the entire medium rent market uniformly. The number of households earning less than $5,000 annually will drop sharply.

---

[2] This estimate was constructed in the following fashion: The initial figure was the housing inventory in the twelve census tracts (5A, 6A, 7A, 7B, 7C, 7D, 8A, 8B, 9A, 9B, 10A, 10B) which contained 2,633 dwelling units in the $60 to $99 rental class in 1950. To this figure were added 200 units that did not report rent or were vacant; minus 400 one-room efficiency units of high quality which do not belong in this group; plus 900 units in the $50-$59 rental class in 1950 that moved into a higher rent bracket by 1957; minus 200 withdrawals, demolitions, and conversions to nonresidential use (according to the Philadelphia City Planning Commission, a total of 350 dwelling units were demolished in central city between 1950 and 1955, and it is estimated that an additional 100 demolitions occurred in 1956-57; slightly less than one-half of the total for 1950-57 were considered to have been drawn from this rent group); plus 200 units added through conversion of structures from single to multi-family use between 1950 and 1957, or through the rehabilitation of multi-family units. The sum of these adjustments was rounded to 3,300.

(Table XIX) This decline will be more than counteracted by an increase in the proportion of households in the upper income ranges, especially those earning $10,000 or more. The net result will be a tendency for the apartments in the high quality ranges of the medium rent bracket to gain in favor at the expense of the cheaper units. In addition, there may be a slight increase in competition between the better rehabilitated units and the new apartment structures.

REPLACEMENT MARKET

As in the case of the high rise apartments, a certain portion of demand for rehabilitated units will emerge as a result of the deterioration of the existing stock in the same area. Unlike the large expensive multi-family structures, however, the inventory of medium-priced units is spread over a large section of center city and among many owners. An estimate of obsolescence and other inventory changes for this portion of the housing stock, therefore, is considerably more difficult. The problem is further complicated by the fact that the rate of filtering in this rent group will be affected by the filtering from above of a number of units now renting for $40 or more per room per month. In Chapter III it was estimated that 950 to 1,250 units will filter into the $20-$35 rent range, and these will have considerable impact on both rents and demand.

For purposes of filtration analysis, the inventory of medium quality units in the downtown area can be grouped into three broad categories. The first consists of structures in or near the fringes of well-maintained or newly improved residential neighborhoods. These units are expected to be enhanced in quality by a considerable amount of new investment and will maintain their position or increase in status as residential improvement in center city continues. The second category contains structures in areas that are not so well located. It is not likely that the future level of improvement or maintenance will prevent further obsolescence of these units and they will continue to deteriorate, or give way to nonresidential use. Some of these will be demolished. The third and final group of structures consists of the floaters which, because of fairly good location and reasonably adequate maintenance, will manage to remain in competition with other medium-priced units in the vicinity. Their relative position in the stock will fluctuate widely as the market shifts from one rate of inventory utilization to another.

It is assumed that all of the units in the first category will retain their relative position in the spectrum of rents. Of the dwelling units in the second category, however, it is estimated that approximately 600 will definitely filter to a lower rent level or be withdrawn from the residential stock. Depending on trends in the housing market, the number of floaters may be reduced by as much as 200 to 300 units. The estimate of total filtering, therefore, is 700 to 900 units. This amount will be more than offset, however, by the 950 to 1,250 units that will filter down from higher rent levels, and the net effect of the filtration will be to augment the supply of dwelling units in the $20 to $35 rent bracket by 250 to 350 units.

CHANGING PREFERENCES

The potential market for rehabilitated apartment units in center city will be augmented by the anticipated shifts in the locational preferences of Philadelphia households. Because of the spread of blight and obsolescence, there is a growing discontent with the environment in many neighborhoods in Philadelphia outside of center city. This factor is of primary importance in the likely change in preferences in favor of the downtown area.

Although the rehabilitated units in Society Hill will not be appreciably different from those available in other parts of center city today, specific demand, directly attributable to Society Hill, will rise as redevelopment proceeds and the site grows in attractiveness and prestige. The absolute number of families who are drawn into the market, however, will be small because the demand for these units comes from a very restricted sector of the population. The survey data revealed that slightly more than one-half of total demand is accounted for by households consisting of single persons or two or more unrelated individuals working in center city and earning $4,000 or more annually. There are at present 40,000 such households in the PSMA. Seventy-five per cent are owners and it is extremely doubtful whether the rehabilitated units would have sufficient glamour or space to attract this group away from their present tenure status.

Thus, one-half of demand is currently drawn from a reservoir of only 10,000 households, less than 1 per cent of the PSMA total. A number of these households already reside in center city; 1,700 in medium-priced units, 1,200 in large apartment structures, and an unknown number in low rent accommodations. It would seem that of the remainder, downtown Philadelphia should be able to attract approximately 100 to 200 families. The maximum number is limited by the availability of many units competitive as to rent and quality in the newer sections of the metropolitan area.

Some additional demand due to change in preferences is likely to come from households consisting of childless married couples in which one or both members are employed in central city. This group now represents one-quarter of the total market for medium-priced rental units in the area. At the present time, there are only 8,000 households of this type in a renter status in the metropolitan area. For this reason, the additions to demand expected to issue from these households will be extremely modest, ranging in the vicinity of 100 to 200 units.

Virtually no families with children are likely to be drawn from other sections of the metropolitan area. In fact, among young downtown renter families the arrival of a child is usually followed by departure from center city sometime before the youngster reaches school age. Even families that do not share the general reluctance to rear their offspring in center city are prompted to leave because of the dearth of moderately priced apartments of adequate size. It is also unlikely that any appreciable change in preference will occur among households that fall outside of the characteristic income bracket or where the principal wage earner is employed outside of the central district.

Total demand stemming from preference changes is estimated, therefore, to be 200 to 400 units. An additional number of families will be drawn into the market by virtue of the attractive prices for units that were recently in the high rent brackets and by reduction in rents of medium quality units affected by this filtration. Although it is not possible to calculate the size of the response to these rent adjustments with precision, it is estimated that the market will be enlarged by as many as 400 to 500 more families, barring a corresponding decline in quality.

SUMMARY

The market potential for center city apartment units renting for $20 to $35 a room is expected to experience a growth of 850 to 1,700 units by 1970. Approximately 60 per cent of the increase will result from a general rise in employment and real income; changing preferences and price changes will account for the remainder of the rise.[3] Some of the potential will, of course, be absorbed by additions to the stock of moderately priced apartments in other sections of center city, but these will not be enough to jeopardize the market in Society Hill.

[3] The method of estimation used for this submarket automatically provides for a vacancy allowance. Since the bulk of the estimated incremental demand is derived by the application of percentage change, the final estimate carries forward to 1970 the current vacancy rate of 5 per cent.

VI

Summary of Future Housing Demand in Center City and the Outlook for Washington Square East

The plan for residential redevelopment and renewal of the Washington Square East area provides for three separate and distinct types of housing accommodations. Approximately 2,000 new apartments, located in predominantly high rise structures, will overlook the Delaware River and the Federal Mall. In addition, 430 new and rehabilitated single family homes ranging in price from $16,000 to $75,000, and about 500 medium rent apartments in rehabilitated structures will be distributed throughout the area. The introduction of these units into the housing inventory will contribute materially to the residential revival of downtown Philadelphia.

A portion of the demand for housing in Society Hill will be generated by its location, environmental characteristics, site plan, and other positive features of the renewal project. These factors, however, play themselves out within the larger context of the center city housing market, one that is sharply distinguished from others in the city. For this reason the analysis has sought to determine the probable expansion of housing demand in the entire central district. These estimates, previously derived, are summarized below. They are followed by a discussion of the implications of the Washington Square East renewal project for center city and the rest of Philadelphia.

THE ESTIMATE OF CENTER CITY DEMAND

According to our calculation for the period 1957-1970, there will be a sizable expansion of demand in center city for each of the three housing types contemplated for Washington Square East. The downtown market will be able to absorb 3,700 to 5,300 apartments in new high rise structures, 850 to 1,700 apartments in smaller converted buildings, and 650 to 1,100 single family homes. Thus, the average annual marketing rate will be approximately 280 to 400 units in the new apartment structures; 100 to 150 units in rehabilitated apartments; and 50 to 90 single family homes. The initial rate of absorption is expected to be considerably higher than the average for the thirteen-year period because of an existing backlog of demand; that is, recent additions to stock have not kept pace with market growth during the mid-1950's.

The market for each of the housing types was estimated by calculating the cumulative effects of five sources of demand for new construction: growth in the number of households, redistribution of employment opportunities, increase in real incomes, replacement of the existing stock, and shifts in the housing preferences of consumers. To this was added the additional construction required to satisfy any backlog of demand and to allow for a vacancy rate that would provide the consumer with a degree of choice without endangering the stability of the market.

On the basis of a series of field interviews it was found that downtown households, be they occupants of high rise apartment houses, single family homes, or the more expensive units in rehabilitated dwellings, are highly homogeneous in composition. Very few of the families have children and even fewer have children of school age. In nine out of ten cases, the head of the household works in center city or is not in the labor force. Over 80 per cent of the households are headed by persons over 35, consist of one or two persons, and have annual incomes considerably above $5,000.

Estimates were made of the change that can be expected in the number of households with these characteristics as a result of general household growth, shifts in the locational distribution of employment, and rising real incomes. These estimates, expressed as percentages for the metropolitan area, were then applied to the total population of center city residents to obtain an approximation of the future demand attributable to general economic expansion. It may be seen in Table XXVII that the growth market will be quite modest, increasing at an average rate of about 2 to 5 per cent annually. The primary impetus to demand will come from the advancement of real income, but the very small anticipated increase in center city employment will be a serious retarding factor.[1]

The growth market will be augmented by demand arising from deterioration, obsolescence, and demolition of a portion of the existing downtown stock. Estimates of the size of the market resulting from the replacement of existing units with new dwellings of superior quality were based on interviews with managers and occupants of downtown apartment structures and on an examination of trends in the volume of conversions and demolitions. It was concluded that filtering to lower rent levels would reach significant proportions among apartment units currently competitive with new construction and will account for roughly one-fourth of total new demand in this sector of the market. By contrast, very few losses are expected in the inventory of good quality single family homes because of the general upgrading of the stock now in progress in nearly every residential block in the area.

A demand factor that has been often discussed but rarely measured in housing market analyses concerns the preferences of consumers for various housing types and locations. In an analysis of an entire city or metropolitan area, this issue is of secondary importance; but when attention is focused on a small and unique slice of the market, as in the case of Washington Square East, the question of preferences assumes considerable significance. In the final analysis, demand in the redevelop-

---

[1] The center city employment forecast takes into account the efforts of the city to stimulate business activity in the CBD.

Table XXVII

SUMMARY OF ESTIMATED RANGE OF DEMAND FOR
DWELLING UNITS IN THE MIDDLE AND UPPER
RENT AND PRICE LEVELS, CENTER CITY
PHILADELPHIA, 1957 TO 1970

	New Apartments ($40/room and up)		Converted Apartments ($20-35/ room)		Single Family Homes ($16,000 and up)	
			Range of Estimate			
	Low	High	Low	High	Low	High
Occupied Dwelling Units, January 1957	3,000	3,000	3,300	3,300	450	450
Incremental Demand, 1957-1970						
Economic Growth						
Households and Employment	200	400	150	410	30	60
Rising Incomes	1,000	1,400	350	740	150	210
Subtotal: Growth	1,200	1,800	500	1,150	180	270
Replacement of Existing Stock	950	1,250	−250	−350	25	50
Changing Preferences	1,000	1,500	600	900	450	810
Backlog of Demand	200	300	—	—	a	a
Change in Vacancy Rate	300	400	—	—	—	—
Total Increase in Demand, 1957-1970	3,650	5,250	850	1,700	655	1,130
Total Demand, January 1970	6,650	8,250	4,150	5,000	1,105	1,580

a Included in changing preferences.

ment area (and in center city as a whole) depends less on general growth factors than on the ability of the area to attract consumers who do not now regard downtown Philadelphia as a place in which they care to live. Accordingly, a calculation was made of the demand that would stem from a shift of consumer preferences in favor of center city living. Although such an estimate cannot be made with a high degree of precision, it appears that demand from this source will be of appreciable magnitude in the middle price ranges ($16,000 to $20,000) of the ownership market and will account for most of the demand generated for centrally located homes in this quality range. (Table XXVII) It will also constitute 30 per cent of the incremental demand for space in the large apartment buildings. In absolute numbers, the importance of preference shifts will be of least consequence in the market for homes selling for more than $25,000 because of the limited number of potential demanders who can afford such expensive accommodations.

THE COMPETITIVE POSITION OF WASHINGTON SQUARE EAST

The redevelopment area, of course, will have to share the market for new construction in downtown Philadelphia with other residential developments. The portion of demand for single family homes and for moderately priced apartments in rehabilitated structures that must be allocated to other sections of the central area is quite small because of the decreasing availability of existing units suitable for conversion or rehabilitation and the shortage of sites for new construction. Likewise, it is not expected that new apartments in other sections of center city will offer serious competition.

The projected demand of 3,700 to 5,300 high rent apartment units for center city during the period 1957-1970 compares with a minimum expansion of supply of approximately 4,000 units. Including the 2,000 units programmed for Society Hill itself, 3,800 are either already under construction or in the advanced stages of planning. Another 200 units are either in the process of rehabilitation or will definitely be raised to a luxury standard in the next three or four years. Although plans have been announced for the construction of more than 1,000 additional units, some of these projects are not expected to materialize, and none will reach the construction and marketing stage prior to the completion or near completion of the Washington Square East project.

The problem of marketing the 2,000 new units in Society Hill, therefore, will not be a serious one. It appears that approximately 1,600 of the potentially competitive units will have been completed and absorbed by the market by the end of 1959 or early 1960. The other 400 (Penn Center House), although still several months away from construction, are already being marketed and most will have been rented before the actual building process commences. Thus the market is not likely to be saturated during the initial phase of construction at Society Hill, and the project should therefore be able to attract 200 to 300 families a year without difficulty from the growing reservoir of families of the type most amenable to a downtown environment.

In addition, the Society Hill redevelopment area, because of its location and environment, will attract some families who would not otherwise be drawn to center city. Moreover, a number of units will be filled by families who now live in other sections of center city, but because of the location of their places of work would strongly prefer to live east of Broad. These two sources of demand comprise a minimum initial market of at least 100 more units annually for Society Hill. It should be emphasized, however, that this level of demand will be contingent upon the rapidity with which the area assumes an appearance befitting its name. If there is protracted delay in clearance and reconstruction, the image of the future will fade and the subsequent pace of renewal will be severely dampened. It is, therefore, necessary to launch a construction program on a scale that will quickly change the face of the area, but will not exceed the sales and rental possibilities in the market.

In summary, the housing market in center city in the coming decade will be characterized by a large increase in demand and an equally impressive expansion of supply. Families seeking expensive accommodations in the area will find a wide range of choice throughout the entire downtown area. In this setting, the residential redevelopment in Washington Square East, if it is to accomplish the purpose for which it was designed, must be programmed with exceptional care and must yield a product competitive in quality and price to anything presently available in downtown Philadelphia. From a marketing point of view, however, there is every indication that the general goals for the area are feasible and that the project can be completed and fully occupied in a reasonable period of time.

IMPLICATIONS FOR THE RENEWAL OF PHILADELPHIA

Although this study was undertaken primarily for the purpose of estimating the demand for certain types of housing accommodations in the central core of Philadelphia, its findings have significant implications for the future of the entire city and, in fact, for most large urban areas throughout the country. As we have indicated in earlier chapters, the households attracted to the central area are small, and are headed by educated and well-to-do members of an adult society. The lives of these people are intimately related to the area. Most of them not only reside, but also work, in the central district. Their friends are nearby and their recreational activities are provided by the downtown life in the city.

By contrast, households with children constitute an extremely small share of center city population. The proportion of these households in the downtown area has diminished very sharply during the past years and from all indications will continue to move in this direction for some time to come. Perhaps the most important reason stems from the fact that most Philadelphia families are persuaded that center city provides an unsuitable environment for rearing children. They feel that the outlying residential areas offer the open space and the type of housing accommodation that is necessary during the child-rearing phase of the family cycle. It also is possible to secure housing space at considerably lower cost in these areas than in center city.

It has frequently been asserted that larger families have avoided center city primarily because suitable accommodations are not available. Middle and upper income households with two or more children require a six or seven-room apartment with three or more bedrooms, and few such apartments exist in the downtown area. The recent marketing experience of several new apartment houses has shown us that even when substantial numbers of large units were made available they rented very slowly, and typically accounted for little more than one out of every twenty units taken in the course of a year.

Many observers feel that the absence of adequate schools is an even more significant deterrent than the lack of large apartment units. This view is incorrect. Our field surveys of a sample of households in the better outlying high rise structures, all of which were located near superior school facilities, revealed that the proportion of families with children in these units was as low as in center city. Apparently, exceedingly few families with children desire apartment living and the provision of educational facilities even of high quality is not likely to alter this preference pattern.

All told, therefore, from the point of view of family inclination or environment or housing accommodations, it is not likely that the number of families with youngsters will increase materially in center city, even after a substantial amount of redevelopment has taken place. It thus appears that center city will be limited to the type of family currently resident in the area, and it is primarily for this reason that the demand for housing accommodations will rise but modestly by 1970. This increase will be sufficient to absorb a major portion of the land available for residential reuse in center city itself, but will not be great enough to support a renewal program in the massive sections of slum and deterioration that lie beyond the central core.

While the housing in these areas is of low quality, the locations are extremely good, for they are within a few minutes' journey of the downtown area. In these areas, moreover, land values are lower and large sections can be redeveloped at moderate densities either in single family use or in garden type apartments. Equally important, unlike center city, substantial portions of the areas can be devoted exclusively to residential and accompanying uses so that the mingling of incompatible activities will be avoided. Hope for a continuation of the regeneration of Philadelphia lies in the renewal programs for these areas, for it is in them that the type of housing and environment can be provided that will attract the household with children. Households of this type constitute the largest sector of housing demand in the entire metropolitan area, and it is through the provision of dwellings that will appeal to them that a material and meaningful return to Philadelphia can be realized.

Even without a large child population, however, the social climate of center city will not suffer. More important, the persons who are presently in the area and those who will be attracted to it, are eminently equipped to produce the type of community leadership necessary to sustain a large metropolis. They are educated, have high incomes, are mature and not burdened with the financial and time costs of rearing young children. They, therefore, are free to devote a substantial portion of their leisure hours to the support of the arts and of various community activities. Moreover, if we view this sector of the population in crass financial terms, we find that they are indeed the municipal comptroller's dream. Their expenditure for rent and consumer goods provides the municipality with substantial real estate and sales taxes. The fact that they tend to occupy fireproof apartment houses means that costs for police and fire protection are minimal. And, what is perhaps more important, the absence of children means that school costs are virtually eliminated. In all, then, we see that although a great surge of population returning from suburban residences to enjoy the convenience and richness of downtown life cannot be expected to materialize in the relatively near future, there is little doubt that substantial numbers of people will continue to live in center city and provide the sustenance necessary to maintain Philadelphia's position as a great urban community.

Appendix

Table I

GROSS RENT PAID BY ALL RENTER HOUSEHOLDS AND BY RENTERS WHO MOVED TO THEIR CURRENT RESIDENCE IN 1955 OR 1956, PHILADELPHIA CITY AND STANDARD METROPOLITAN AREA, DECEMBER 1956

	(Per cent)			
	All Renters		Recent Renters	
Gross Rent	PSMA	Philadelphia	PSMA	Philadelphia
Less than $20	0.5	0.6	0.5	0.4
20-29	3.8	4.8	3.2	5.2
30-39	9.3	11.9	7.1	10.2
40-49	18.2	20.4	15.2	20.9
50-59	20.0	22.7	18.9	19.8
60-69	15.8	16.6	17.5	19.8
70-79	10.8	8.7	11.4	10.9
80-89	6.8	4.6	6.8	3.6
90-99	4.6	3.9	4.7	2.9
100-119	6.6	3.4	10.9	4.7
120 and up	3.6	2.4	3.8	1.6
TOTAL	100.0	100.0	100.0	100.0

Source: *1956 National Housing Inventory*, U.S. Bureau of the Census; unpublished data.

Table II

VALUE OF SINGLE FAMILY DWELLING UNITS OF ALL
OWNER OCCUPANTS AND OF HOUSEHOLDS THAT
PURCHASED HOMES IN 1955 AND 1956
PHILADELPHIA CITY AND STANDARD
METROPOLITAN AREA, DECEMBER 1956

	(Per cent)			
	All Owners		Recent Buyers	
Value	PSMA	Philadelphia	PSMA	Philadelphia
Less than $4,000	2.7	4.0	1.8	2.4
4,000-5,999	9.5	13.3	7.3	13.1
6,000-7,999	15.7	28.3	8.3	20.4
8,000-9,999	15.5	21.4	10.5	16.7
10,000-11,999	18.2	14.3	17.8	14.8
12,000-14,999	15.9	10.2	23.3	15.5
15,000-19,999	13.8	6.3	17.5	15.6
20,000 or more	8.7	2.2	13.5	1.5
TOTAL	100.0	100.0	100.0	100.0

Source: *1956 National Housing Inventory*, U.S. Bureau of the Census; unpublished data.

Table III

CHARACTERISTICS OF RESIDENTS OF CENTER CITY HIGH RENT APARTMENTS AND MEDIUM AND HIGH PRICE SINGLE FAMILY HOMES COMPARED WITH ALL HOUSEHOLDS IN PHILADELPHIA CITY AND PHILADELPHIA STANDARD METROPOLITAN AREA, 1957

	(Per cent)				
	Downtown Philadelphia			PSMA	Philadelphia
	High Priced Apartments	Single Family Units			
		Owners	Renters		
A. Number of Persons in Household					
One and Two	87.2	60.8	67.4	36.7	43.8
Three	12.0	27.8	19.6	21.2	20.5
Four or More	0.8	11.4	13.0	42.1	35.7
TOTAL	100.0	100.0	100.0	100.0	100.0
B. Age of Head of Household					
Under 25	—	—	9.1	2.7	3.0
25-34	2.2	8.1	45.4	19.5	15.3
35-44	12.4	14.9	18.3	24.6	23.7
45-54	27.9	32.4	9.1	20.5	21.1
55-64	25.1	31.1	4.5	17.5	20.0
65 and over	32.4	13.5	13.6	15.2	16.9
TOTAL	100.0	100.0	100.0	100.0	100.0
C. Type of Household					
Head, wife—no children and no additional adults	44.8	35.4	17.4	21.8	23.3
Head, wife—no children, one or more additional adults	9.6	19.0	—	9.3	10.1
Head, wife—children, all under six	2.9	10.1	21.7	13.0	9.1

Table III (Continued)

	(Per cent)				
	Downtown Philadelphia			PSMA Philadelphia	
	High Priced Apartments	Single Family Units			
		Owners	Renters		
C. Type of Household					
Head, wife—children, at least one child six or over	0.8	3.8	6.5	31.0	26.5
Single, widow, etc., no children	39.7	30.4	52.3	18.5	23.4
Widowed, divorced, etc., with children	2.2	1.3	2.1	6.4	7.6
TOTAL	100.0	100.0	100.0	100.0	100.0
D. Household Income					
Under $5,000	4.7	20.7	20.0	48.9	57.6
$5,000-7,499	44.9	27.6	14.3	29.9	28.2
$7,500-9,999	—	6.9	17.1	11.3	7.2
Over $10,000	50.4	44.8	48.6	9.9	7.0
TOTAL	100.0	100.0	100.0	100.0	100.0
E. Occupation					
Professional, technical	17.9	41.0	52.2	10.5	6.8
Managers, officials	39.9	20.5	11.5	9.1	8.6
Clerical, sales	15.0	14.1	16.1	10.8	13.2
Craftsmen, foremen	3.7	2.6	—	17.7	17.3
Operatives, laborers	—	—	—	18.4	22.1
Service	—	7.7	9.1	6.3	9.0
Does not work	23.5	14.1	11.1	27.2	23.0
TOTAL	100.0	100.0	100.0	100.0	100.0
F. Place of Employment					
Center City	66.5	72.2	71.1	13.6	16.9
Varying Location	2.2	—	8.9	8.3	9.0
Does not work	23.5	14.1	11.1	27.2	23.0
All others	7.8	13.7	8.9	50.9	51.1
TOTAL	100.0	100.0	100.0	100.0	100.0

Table III (Continued)

	(Per cent)				
	Downtown Philadelphia			PSMA Philadelphia	
	High Priced Apartments	Single Family Units			
		Owners	Renters		
G. Sex of head					
Male	61.3	74.7	78.3	83.4	78.6
Female	38.7	25.3	21.7	16.6	21.4
TOTAL	100.0	100.0	100.0	100.0	100.0
H. Car Ownership[a]					
Yes	63.9	87.0	80.0	72.8	57.0
No	36.1	13.0	20.0	27.2	43.0
TOTAL	100.0	100.0	100.0	100.0	100.0
I. Previous Residence[b]					
Center City	30.4	52.6	71.7	⎰ 51.6	90.0
Other Philadelphia	44.0	29.5	2.2	⎱	
Suburbs	16.8	11.5	2.2	35.6	3.0
Outside PSMA	8.8	6.4	23.9	12.8	7.0
TOTAL	100.0	100.0	100.0	100.0	100.0

[a] Apartment house data refer only to Rittenhouse Plaza, Rittenhouse Claridge, and 2601 Parkway.

[b] Data for Philadelphia and PSMA refer to households that moved in 1955 and 1956.

Source: Figures for center city residents are from field surveys by ACTION and the Institute for Urban Studies. Data for the city of Philadelphia and the Philadelphia Standard Metropolitan Area are from unpublished tabulations of the *1956 National Housing Inventory*, U.S. Bureau of the Census.

Table IV

LENGTH OF RESIDENCE IN CENTER CITY,
OCCUPANTS OF HIGH RENT APARTMENTS
AND MEDIUM AND HIGH PRICE
SINGLE FAMILY HOMES, 1957

Length of Residence	(Per cent)		
	Apartment Residents	Single Family Home	
		Owners	Renters
Less than 1 year	11.2	10.2	39.1
1 yr.-1 yr. 11 mos.	8.9	9.0	23.9
2 yrs.-4 yrs. 11 mos.	27.5	11.5	19.6
5-10 yrs.	31.4	35.9	8.7
Over 10 yrs.	21.0	33.4	8.7
TOTAL	100.0	100.0	100.0

Source: Field surveys by ACTION and by the Institute for Urban Studies.

Table V

TYPE OF STRUCTURE OF PREVIOUS RESIDENCE, CURRENT OCCUPANTS OF HIGH RENT APARTMENTS AND MEDIUM AND HIGH PRICE SINGLE FAMILY HOMES, CENTER CITY PHILADELPHIA, 1957

| | (Per cent) | | |
| | | Single Family Home | |
Previous Residence	Apartment Residents	Owners	Renters
Single Family or Duplex	53.3	56.0	22.7
Apartment	46.7	44.0	77.3
TOTAL	100.0	100.0	100.0

Source: Field surveys by ACTION and by the Institute for Urban Studies.

Table VI

PROPORTION OF RESIDENTS OF CENTER CITY HIGH RENT APARTMENTS AND MEDIUM AND HIGH PRICE SINGLE FAMILY HOMES WHO OWN OR RENT A SECOND DWELLING UNIT IN ANOTHER AREA, 1957

| | (Per cent) | | |
| | | Single Family Home | |
Second Dwelling Unit	Apartment Residents	Owner	Renter
Yes	8.2	6.6	7.5
No	91.8	93.4	92.5
TOTAL	100.0	100.0	100.0

Source: Field surveys by ACTION and by the Institute for Urban Studies.

Table VII

EXTENT OF SATISFACTION WITH DWELLING UNIT AND
LOCATION, RESIDENTS OF HIGH RENT APARTMENTS
AND MEDIUM AND HIGH PRICE SINGLE FAMILY
HOMES, CENTER CITY PHILADELPHIA, 1957

| | | (Per cent) | |
| | | Single Family Homes | |
Extent of Satisfaction	Apartment Residents	Owners	Renters
Dwelling Unit			
Very Satisfied	94.4	88.8	82.6
Mildly Satisfied	4.8	7.5	8.7
Indifferent	0.8	1.2	2.2
Mildly Dissatisfied	0	2.5	6.5
Very Dissatisfied	0	0	0
TOTAL	100.0	100.0	100.0
Location			
Very Satisfied	97.6	90.1	84.8
Mildly Satisfied	2.4	5.0	8.7
Indifferent	0	1.2	0
Mildly Dissatisfied	0	1.2	6.5
Very Dissatisfied	0	2.5	0
TOTAL	100.0	100.0	100.0

Source: Field surveys by ACTION and by the Institute for Urban Studies.

Table VIII

ADVANTAGES AND DISADVANTAGES OF LIVING IN CENTER CITY EXPRESSED BY RESIDENTS OF CENTER CITY HIGH RENT APARTMENTS PHILADELPHIA, 1957

	Per cent of Respondents Mentioning Characteristic[a]
Advantages	
Proximity to shopping and cultural activities	54
Proximity to work	37
Proximity to center city activities (type not specified)	30
Proximity to inter- and intra-urban transportation facilities	20
Scenic views and nearby green space	10
Friendly and interesting people	9
Proximity to friends	8
Safety	8
Other[b]	18
None	3
Disadvantages	
None	56
Dirt and noise	16
Lack of adequate parking facilities	8
Lack of green space	6
Other[c]	14

[a] Some respondents mentioned more than one advantage.

[b] Includes: service and conveniences in the building, privacy, proximity to schools, apartments all on one floor, no parking problems, no need to shovel snow.

[c] Includes: expensive food purchases, not near friends or relatives, form of travel to work objectionable, dangerous neighborhood, have to use taxi to travel, dislike pavements, annoyed by friends from suburbs, kosher food not available, not enough green and trees, transportation to other parts of city not good, dislike of people in neighborhood, rent too high, too far from doctor.

Source: Field surveys by ACTION and by the Institute for Urban Studies.

Index

Date Due

FEB 17 '65		
MAY 2 '67		
JAN 8 '68		
JUL 19 '68		
DEC 11 '69		
MAY 2 '69		

Demco 293-5